# Web-Based Instruction

## A Practical Guide for Online Courses

James Van Keuren

LB1044.87.V36 2006
Van Keuren, James.
Web-based instruction : a
practical guide for online
courses
Lanham, Md. : Rowman &
Littlefield Education, 2006.

Rowman & Littlefield Education
Lanham, Maryland • Toronto • Oxford
2006

Published in the United States of America
by Rowman & Littlefield Education
A Division of Rowman & Littlefield Publishers, Inc.
A wholly owned subsidiary of The Rowman & Littlefield Publishing
Group, Inc.
4501 Forbes Boulevard, Suite 200, Lanham, Maryland 20706
www.rowmaneducation.com

PO Box 317
Oxford
OX2 9RU, UK

British Library Cataloguing in Publication Information Available

**Library of Congress Cataloging-in-Publication Data**

Van Keuren, James.
  Web-based instruction : a practical guide for online courses / James Van
Keuren.
     p. cm.
  Includes bibliographical references.
  ISBN-13: 978-1-57886-442-3 (hardcover : alk. paper)
  ISBN-13: 978-1-57886-443-0 (pbk. : alk. paper)
  ISBN-10: 1-57886-442-9 (hardcover : alk. paper)
  ISBN-10: 1-57886-443-7 (pbk. : alk. paper)
  1. Web-based instruction. 2. College teaching—Aids and devices. I.
Title.
  LB1044.87.V36 2006
  378.1'7344678—dc22                                   2006003114

$\infty$ ™ The paper used in this publication meets the minimum requirements
of American National Standard for Information Sciences—Permanence of
Paper for Printed Library Materials, ANSI/NISO Z39.48-1992.
Manufactured in the United States of America.

# Contents

# Introduction

This guide is designated to take the frustration out of designing and implementing a Web-based and/or Web-assisted instructional delivery approach. The guide has a "how to" approach, requiring only that you have the confidence, desire, and patience to use alternative instructional delivery approaches.

The guide is organized into eight chapters. Chapter 1 lays out some practical considerations that need to be reviewed before considering using Web-based and/or Web-assisted instructional delivery approaches. Chapter 2 discusses how to win student respect and trust when using alternative instructional delivery approaches. Chapter 3 delineates the support systems that are needed to successfully implement alternative instructional delivery approaches. Chapter 4 discusses the steps in transitioning from the classroom-based approach to using technology as an alternative instructional delivery tool. Chapter 5 outlines and provides examples of course designs that make sense. Chapter 6 illustrates and gives examples of interactive assignments. Chapter 7 provides student feedback examples and how they can be used to improve and strengthen instructional delivery approaches. Chapter 8 discusses why it is important to be accountable to the students and the institution that you serve. The appendices provide examples of a self-evaluation form for potential online students, an institutional policy for an alternative instructional delivery program, questions that students might ask about Web-based courses, a student evaluation instrument and an online technology questionnaire; the glossary defines the key terms used in the guide.

# 1

# Why a Guide?

## BACKGROUND

The system of higher education, like the public system, was designed to meet the needs of the industrial age and now is shifting to meet the needs of an information age. At the higher education level, a need exists to develop new ways to deliver instruction to students.

Judith Boettcher (1999) believes that institutions of higher education when approaching online learning or distance learning need to customize learning for students to make it available anytime, anywhere. She believes that "interactive online learning is an educational philosophy for designing interactive, responsive, and valid information and learning opportunities to be delivered to learners at a time, place, and in appropriate forms convenient to learners" (p. 1).

Distance education has teachers changing from being the repository of all knowledge to being guides and mentors who help students through information made available by technology and interactive communication. In an article titled "Emerging Technology in Distance Learning," it was brought out that technological advances have created a paradigm shift from student-filled, single teacher-directed classes to more teacherless, boundaryless, timeless learning (Bingham, Davis & Moore, 1996).

The shift in instructional approaches has stimulated an interest in higher education to look at alternative instructional delivery approaches such as Web-based and Web-assisted instruction. It is a paradigm shift on the part of student and instructor, especially as it pertains to not having face-to-face contact, access to a computer, and the use of a compatible Web browser. This approach provides the student with the opportunity to learn at any time, any place because the instructional walls and boundaries are eliminated with the instructor still able to maintain the integrity of the course content.

## STRENGTHS

The Alternative Instructional Delivery Committee at Ashland University found that there were certain strengths inherit in successful Web-based and Web-assisted courses. The committee believed that the strengths outlined below were positive points for faculty members to consider as they contemplated whether or not they should use Web-based and Web-assisted instructional delivery approaches (Strengths and Weakness of Alternatively Delivered Courses, 2001).

- Accent on the Individual: If each student sends work on a regular basis, and the instructor enforces this, the student cannot hide. Typed work requires thought and editing; putting one's thoughts "on the record" motivates a student to think before writing. Reading the work takes considerable time for the instructor; neither the instructor nor the student should think that Web-based or Web-assisted courses are easier.
- Motivation: A self-motivated student can shine in his/her written work by taking advantage of scheduling flexibility.
- Evaluation: The instructor should receive more written work than in a traditional classroom-based course, which serves as an excellent base to evaluate student performance.
- Study Methods: The student has time to formulate proper, well thought out answers and has the opportunity to edit and revise postings before sending. This results in responses that are reasoned and reflective.

- Access: With the exception of entire-class chat activities, students can work online at any time of the day or night. Interaction and discussion via discussion threads can occur many times during the week, not just for a few hours in a weekly classroom session. Online instruction is ideal for the student with a strong visual learning style.

- Enhancing Access to Course Related Materials: Students can easily refer class members to useful Web sites or articles by using hyperlinks imbedded within discussion postings. The ability to attach files, including images, to postings makes it possible for students and instructors to share resources that would be difficult to distribute in a regular classroom setting.

- Academic Quality: Students remain constantly involved with the course if regular participation in threaded discussions is required. Interaction through threaded discussions can occur many times a week, not just a few hours in a week classroom session. The first step, as an instructor, is to determine if you want to make the leap from face-to-face instruction to Web-based or Web-assisted instruction. You must believe that you can actualize the points the Ashland University Instructional Delivery Committee outlines. The instructor also needs to feel comfortable using the computer as an instructional delivery tool.

## ADULT LEARNERS

The challenge I faced was to incorporate Web-based and Web-assisted instructional delivery approaches with adult learners. In an article titled "Andragogy: The Teaching and Learning of Adults," it is pointed out that children come to school with limited experiences, while adults have a great deal of life experience upon which additional knowledge is more easily established (Noren, 1997). Knowles

(1990) believes that the teaching and learning of adults is different and that one must think of the adult learner in the following manner:

- Adults need to know why they need to learn something before undertaking to learn it.
- Adults have a self-concept of being responsible for their own decisions and their own lives.
- Adults come into an education activity with both a greater volume and a different quality of experience from youths.
- Adults become ready to learn those things they need to know and be able to do in order to cope effectively with their real-life situations.
- Adults are motivated to devote energy to learn something to the extent that they perceive that it will help them perform tasks or deal with problems that they confront in their life situations.
- While adults are responsive to some external motivators (better jobs, promotions, higher salaries, and the like), the most potent motivators are internal pressures (desire for increased job satisfaction, self-esteem, quality of life, and so forth) (pp. 57–63).

In structuring Web-based and Web-assisted instructional delivery approaches, Knowles' descriptors about adult learners must be taken into consideration given that the online learning environment is a shift from being teacher-centered to student-centered, where the learning takes place anytime and anyplace. It means adjusting instructional delivery approaches with adult learners who have not been in the classroom for a while and do not have updated technology skills.

## PRINCIPLES OF GOOD PRACTICE

The debate continues over what works and does not work in a Web-based and Web-assisted instructional learning environment. As one entertains the idea of using technology as an instructional tool, consideration needs to be given to good teaching practices. The Ohio Learning Network, in the following table, illustrates how the "Principles of Good Practice" can interact with technology.

To implement the "Principles of Good Practice" the instructor must take into consideration the attitudes of the students and their

**Table 1.1. Principles of Good Practice**

| Principles of Good Practice | Role Technology Can Play |
|---|---|
| Encourage contact between students and faculty members. | Computer-mediated communication provides for faster, more open and more reflective communication. |
| Develop reciprocity and cooperation among students. | Computer-mediated communication facilitates group interaction, problem solving and building communities. |
| Use active learning techniques. | Technology-based simulations allow for greater interactivity and student manipulation, and primary resources in digital format enhance student scholarly work. |
| Give prompt feedback. | Computer-mediated communication provides considerable avenues for prompt and reflective feedback. |
| Emphasize time on task. | Technology provides new opportunities for creating new forms of mediated environments which can provide structure and engage the students. |
| Communicate high expectations. | Computer-mediated environments offer instructors a variety of avenues for demonstrating and conveying high expectations. Furthermore, these environments can provide dramatic shifts in the audience, which can foster higher expectations from student work. |
| Respect diverse talents and ways of learning. | Technology provides the means for instructors to build multiple pathways to learning within the same course by allowing content learning and discussion in multiple ways. |

*Source: Quality learning in Ohio and at a distance, 2002.*

individual learning styles. Patience on the part of both instructor and student is a key element in successfully implementing these principles. The instructor needs to internalize that quality and academic rigor are parts of the course requirements. The course syllabus should reflect the same kind of academic rigor that would be found in the traditional classroom setting.

## QUESTIONS TO BE ANSWERED

The instructor, in order to successfully implement Web-based and Web-assisted instructional delivery approaches, must be able to answer the following questions:

- Can I make the switch from face-to-face instruction to Web-based and Web-assisted instruction?
- What is my comfort level using technology as an instructional tool?
- What kind of training do I need?
- Is there monetary support for developing Web-based and Web-assisted courses?
- What is the technical support available at my institution?
- What kind of hardware and software do I need at home and in my office?
- Can I convert my course into a Web-based and Web-assisted format and maintain quality and academic rigor?
- Can I create a climate that encourages students to learn?

If, as an instructor, you feel uncomfortable with the answers to these questions, then it may not be appropriate to pursue a Web-based and Web-assisted instructional delivery approach. On the other hand, if the questions can be answered with assurance that the courses will contain quality and academic rigor, then you are ready to move forward with Web-based and Web-assisted instructional delivery approaches.

Now let's go on an exciting journey covering how to integrate Web-based and Web-assisted instructional delivery approaches into your repertoire of instructional delivery strategies.

## CONCLUSION

Web-based and Web-assisted instructional delivery approaches provide students with the opportunity to learn anytime and anyplace. If structured correctly alternative instructional delivery approaches will be able to meet the needs of a mobile student population. This chapter examined the strengths of Web-based and Web-assisted courses, the needs of adult learners, principles of good practices integrated with instructional technology and whether or not as an instructor you are ready to pursue alternative instructional delivery approaches. This chapter provides background for the sequential chapters that delineate a practical guide for developing Web-based and Web-assisted instructional delivery approaches.

## SIGNIFICANT POINTS

- This is a paradigm shift in using technology as an alternative instructional delivery tool.
- Strengths: Accent on the individual, motivation, evaluation, study methods, access, and enhancing access to course-related materials and academic quality.
- Adult learners bring life experiences to the class.
- Principles of good practice should be integrated with technology tools.
- Determining whether or not the instructor is ready to pursue Web-based and Web-assisted instructional delivery approaches.

# 2

# Winning Student Respect and Trust

## BACKGROUND

The challenge for the instructor of Web-based and Web-assisted courses is to win student respect and trust. This may sound like an easy task to accomplish but in reality it is difficult to do, because you are shifting from face-to-face to a Web-based or Web-assisted instructional learning environment. The shift in the instructional approach can create fear and anxiety about the unknown on the part of the student. The student anxiety comes from a loss of personal contact between the student and faculty member and the students themselves. Weiss (2000) believed that in order for online instructional delivery to be successful it must become a personal experience for students and faculty members. She stated, "If an online course is handled in the proper way, the personality of the professor and camaraderie of fellow students can be achieved even in the absence of face-to-face contact. However, this will not happen automatically. The course must be taught in a way that cultivates relationships; if this is done, the professor and students will be regarded with a satisfying personal relationship despite the distance that separates them" (p. 51).

## FOUNDATION FOR SUCCESS

In order to establish positive personal relationships, the instructor must eliminate the student's anxiety and uncertainty in taking Web-based and Web-assisted courses. This anxiety level can also hold true for the instructor who has committed to changing his or her instructional delivery approaches. Taking a proactive approach in answering the following questions will assist in establishing a foundation for winning student respect and trust.

### Is the Student Ready for Web-Based and Web-Assisted Courses?

This can be accomplished through an online preliminary assessment (Appendix A) and through personal interviews. The preliminary assessment tool and personal interviews can assist the instructor in predicting whether or not students are going to have difficulty taking Web-based or Web-assisted courses. It is only fair to let the students know up front about the difficulties they might encounter.

### How Do You Work with Students Who Have the Preconceived Notion That an Online Course Is Not Going to Be User-Friendly?

As an instructor you must spend quality time with the students during orientation or additional information sessions to ensure that they have a comfort level with using the course technology tools. Some institutions of higher education have the students go through a technology orientation session prior to taking an online course. The students need to know the course requirements for software and hardware. In my course outlines I include the following statement:

> Be sure you have the ability to access a computer that is connected to the Internet. Some of the required readings and work will be available through the Internet on the weekly schedule of assignments. You will need to know how to download files such as Adobe.pdf documents and how to print documents from the computer screen. You will also need a telephone modem connection speed of 56.6 Bauds/Kbs or

higher and a Web browser (Netscape 4.7 or higher or Internet Explorer 5.0 or higher). Microsoft Works 5.0 programs are not compatible with the programs on campus. Also, you should check as to whether or not your computer system has a firewall that would not allow you to use the chat room feature.

This statement is a part of the description in the course schedule that is distributed to the students. Also, the discussion and the understanding of the technology side of the course requirements will eliminate the "I did not know" statement on the part of the student.

Some institutions of higher education have pretraining sessions for students taking Web-based and Web-assisted courses, but I have found that most students come to class with adequate technology skills and are able to adjust to the WebCt course design I use in my classes.

I take time during my class to explain to the students how they can access the online course content and the communications tools, such as the bulletin board, private e-mail system, chat room, assignment drop box, and grade-recording system. We spend time in class posting messages and doing threaded discussions on the bulletin board, exchanging e-mails, and practicing chat room discussions. I have the students practice test assignments so they get use to downloading assignments to the assignment drop box. For those students who have not developed a comfort level with using the technology tools, I will schedule an alternative class day to give them the opportunity to practice using the WebCt technology tools.

This extra effort to assist students in feeling comfortable with using technology as an instructional tool will pay dividends in the end, especially when it comes time for student evaluations.

## How Do You Work with Students Who Have Difficulty Making the Transition to Web-Based and Web-Assisted Instruction?

Even though you have done what you believe is an adequate screening process, you will encounter students who are have difficulty making the shift from face-to-face instruction to Web-based or Web-assisted instruction. This kind of student will need some handholding.

My classes are structured to include at least four face-to-face class-room sessions with two of the classes scheduled early in the term. I use the course e-mail system, bulletin board postings, and telephone calls to stay connected to my students. I have found the bulletin board to be an effective communication and information tool where the students and instructor can exchange thoughts on questions posted about class assignments or technology problems. The course e-mail system provides students with the opportunity to exchange comments with the instructor on a private basis. I make it a practice to call those students who I sense are having difficulty with the on-line course format; past experience tells me they may not success-fully complete the course. In the most extreme cases, I have made personal visits to these students at their place of work.

### What If the Students Cannot Access the University Server?

Students often panic when they cannot access the university server. They should be aware that if there is a problem connecting to the university server, they can contact the university help desk or call me at home or work. Also, they can contact me through the class private e-mail or my personal e-mail.

### What If the Students Cannot Access the Assignment Links?

Again, I have instructed my students to contact me at any time and any place. They have my work and home telephone numbers. During the first several weeks of class, a few of the students will contact me at home or work, where I can go online and talk them though their problems. I give the students a comfort level that they can re-ceive assistance day or night.

### How Do You Maintain Timely Feedback to the Students?

I found in Web-based and Web-assisted instructional learning envi-ronments that students desire instant feedback to their e-mails, assignments, and bulletin board postings. I use the course private e-mail system to stay in touch with the students. Also, bulletin board postings are an effective method of informing the class about course information, which often ends up in threaded discussions. During the first few weeks of class, I call the students that I sense are still unsure about the Web-based and Web-assisted instructional delivery format. I e-mail and telephone students as an integral way to keep open the lines of communication. Since teaching Web-based and Web-assisted courses, I probably communicate better with students than I did when I was in the traditional classroom setting.

## How Do You Convince the Students There is a Time Commitment in Doing the Course Work?

Often students have the notion that taking an online course means less work than they would have in the traditional classroom setting. In my early Web-based courses, I had several students who never completed their course work because they did not realize that there was as much or more work in the online classroom setting. One remedy to keep students current is to structure the assignment drop box, where they can only submit their work on a due date. In a paper titled "Non-completion in Alternative Delivery Courses: A Two-year Comparative Study," by Bali, Moorman, Wingreen, and Adams (2001), it was found that the pressures of job and family were the most significant reasons why students failed to complete online courses. Other reasons were difficulty with content, faculty members, administration/technical staff, health, length of course, and cost.

## Functional versus Dysfunctional Classroom Setting

Figure 2.1 depicts a dysfunctional classroom setting where the faculty member has not made the course expectations clear and thus the students are unclear about the learning outcomes of the course. Figure 2.2, on the other hand, illustrates a functional classroom setting

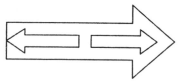

**Figure 2.1.   Dysfunctional Classroom Setting**

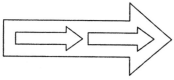

**Figure 2.2.   Functional Classroom Setting**

with clear course expectations where the students and instructor are aligned as to the learning outcomes of the course. Peter Senge (1990) would say that Figure 2.2 is an illustration of where wasted energy has been converted into a commonality of purpose and shared vision.

The worst-case scenario in the Web-based and Web-assisted instructional design is to create a dysfunctional classroom setting. The instructor who is leading the instructional change process must be able to create a common synergy with the students to ensure that there are clear course expectations. A functional Web-based and Web-assisted classroom environment is a good indication that you have gained the students' respect and trust.

## WHAT DO THE STUDENTS THINK?

In a Web-assisted class, I asked the students what should an instructor do to gain the respect and trust of the students? The students identified instructor accessibility and feedback, ability to demonstrate how to use course technology tools, and content expertise as key factors in gaining their respect and trust.

By far instructor feedback was the most common comment by students. The students believed that the instructor should hold face-to-face classes during the beginning of the course, provide quick responses to e-mails and grading of assignments, hold regular office hours, have direct conversation with individual students in addition to whole group instruction, and be accessible through private e-mail and the telephone in case of problems.

The students believed that the instructor must demonstrate a knowledge and understanding of how to adapt and use the Web-based and Web-assisted instructional delivery approaches to meet the learning outcomes of the course. The students thought that the instructor should provide online resources that present the course in a nonthreatening manner and in a format that gives them a comfort level for doing their work.

Finally, the students indicated that Web-based and Web-assisted instructional delivery approaches should not overshadow the fact that the instructor must be a content expert first and foremost. In a Web-based and Web-assisted instructional learning environment, the instructor should be able to integrate the content with the technology tools. One student commented that "developing credibility and a level of competence regarding the material so students don't feel that the alternative methods are simply designed to take the load off the teacher" could gain respect and trust.

The bottom line is that students believe that the course should be designed to create a community environment where the participants are able to work together and share their work on the Web.

## CONCLUSION

Online assessments and interviews assist in determining those students who may not be ready to take Web-based or Web-assisted courses. These types of screenings will eliminate potential frustrations on the part of disgruntled students.

Winning student respect and trust in a Web-based and Web-assisted instructional learning environment takes a commitment from the instructor to communicate with the students. It means that the instructor must find ways of eliminating student anxiety levels when moving from face-to-face instruction to a Web-based and Web-assisted instructional learning environment. The most effective way of winning student respect and trust is to provide different avenues for the students to contact the instructor anytime and anyplace. Repeated comments by the students centered on timely instructor feedback and the instructor's ability to demonstrate how to use the course technologies as important factors in creating a reassuring and comfortable learning environment.

Students in a Web-based and Web-assisted instructional learning environment want an instructor who is a content expert and who has the competence to demonstrate how to use course technology tools. It is important that the instructor maintains a functional online classroom environment by providing clear course expectations where students and instructor are aligned as to the learning outcomes of the course. A dysfunctional learning environment will occur when students say that the course expectations were unclear and that they did not receive timely feedback on their questions and course work. When this happens, you will lose their respect and trust.

## SIGNIFICANT POINTS

- Student screening can be done through preliminary assessment tools and personal interviews.
- Students need to know the course requirements for software and hardware.
- Structure face-to-face contacts with the students during the first few weeks of class.
- Provide the opportunity for students to contact the instructor at any time and any place.

- Provide instant feedback to student e-mails, assignments, bulletin board postings, and phone calls.
- Enforce time commitments for students to furnish their assignments.
- Demonstrate how to use the course technology tools.
- Be a content expert.
- Create a functional classroom setting by providing clear course expectations where the students and the instructor are aligned as to the learning outcomes of the course.

# 3

## Support Systems

### BACKGROUND

The key to successful Web-based and Web-assisted courses is organizational support for faculty members and faculty support for the student learners. Technical support for faculty members and students is critical in developing and delivery of Web-based and Web-assisted courses.

In maintaining a viable Web-based and Web-assisted instructional learning environment, there has to be a three-prong approach. First, there must be organizational support for alternative instructional delivery approaches, technical assistance, infrastructure, and course design and development. Second, there should be faculty support in the form of technical assistance and monetary support for course design and development. Third, a technical support system for students should be established to provide the same kind of service as would be provided to the traditional student population. If this three-prong approach is not developed, the Web-based and Web-assisted instructional delivery approaches are doomed to failure.

### ORGANIZATIONAL COMMITMENT

In formulating a distance education program there should be a policy that includes but is not limited to definitions, stipulations, course eligibility and training requirements, course development funds, course ownership, course review, class size and meeting requirements, tuition, and identification of the department that will be administrating the distance education programs.

The Ashland University Alternative Instructional Delivery Committee developed the organizational policies found in Appendix B (Ashland University Policy for Alternative Instructional Delivery, 2004). The policy was designed to provide university faculty members the opportunity to reach a wider student audience through the use of alternative instructional delivery approaches. It includes a framework that provides guidance to faculty members who are interested in using Web-based and Web-assisted instructional delivery approaches. Most important, it provides financial incentives for faculty members and departments to use alternative instructional delivery approaches.

## FACULTY SUPPORT

If faculty members are interested in pursuing Web-based and Web-assisted instructional delivery approaches, they should look to their informational technology departments to determine if there is a support system in place. DeNigris and Witchel (2000) stated:

> Students and facilitators both will drop from distance training programs over the Internet if they are stressed by the lack of support or inadequacies of the system to fulfill learning objectives. Stress occurs when we perceive that something is standing in our way to achieve a valued outcome. Good online training is a valued outcome by both the learner and teacher. The outcome cannot be achieved if both are distracted by an infrastructure that doesn't facilitate this goal or if technical support is lacking. (p. 3)

There is not a magical formula for developing a faculty support system, but at the minimum there must be a professional development component that provides faculty members the necessary training to succeed in the distance education instructional learning environment. The policy that the Ashland University Alternative Instructional Delivery Committee developed was committed to faculty training, faculty compensation, course development funds, and course material ownership.

I have advised faculty members who are considering using Web-based and Web-assisted instructional approaches to talk with their peers about what they have done with their online courses. Also, I have suggested that prior to doing a training session, faculty members meet with the department of informational technology staff to ascertain whether or not Web-based and Web-assisted instructional delivery approaches are appropriate teaching venues.

The next step for the faculty member interested in using Web-based and Web-assisted instructional delivery approaches would be to obtain training. Ashland University places the responsibility on the faculty member to register and pursue the training to teach Web-based or Web-assisted courses. The university provides an online training calendar with guides for software, computer, and Internet use, plus a Web/Ct manual for Web-based and Web-assisted courses.

The training component, at the very least, must be structured to ensure that the faculty members become skilled is using technology tools and are able to change the course design when needed. The faculty member, before moving to a Web-based and Web-assisted instructional learning environment, must have a comfort level with using technology tools in the classroom and believe that there is an adequate infrastructure and support system in place. The worst-case scenario would be to have frustrated students who believe that they are in a dysfunctional classroom setting.

## STUDENT SUPPORT

Web-based and Web-assisted courses are not for everyone. This approach requires a paradigm shift on the part of the student, especially as it pertains to not having face-to-face contact with other students and the instructor. In order to assist students in the transition to the online course environment, there needs to be a strong support system in place. Because there is such a dependence on written skills, DeNigris and Witchel (2000) suggest that the students should have, at the very least, the following qualifications:

- The ability to read well.
- The ability to write well.
- The ability to express thoughts and emotions in writing.
- Realistic expectations of the time commitment to learning through the Internet or online.
- Sufficient training on the software before starting the course (p. 4).

I have found that most of my graduate students have very good writing skills and have been able to fulfill the qualifications listed by DeNigrus and Witchel. Also, as an instructor, I have impressed on the students that there needs to be a time commitment to the course work or they will find themselves falling behind until they are unable to catch up. I always put a scare into the class by giving examples of students who never finished the course work and thus ended up failing the class. This seems to prompt the students into action.

It is important that the administration has a commitment to technical support that is available to the students either through a help desk or online. This proactive approach will augment the instructor's technical assistance during the progression of the course. Once again it is important to have the students develop a comfort level of moving from face-to-face instruction to a Web-based and Web-assisted instructional learning environment.

It is important to develop a viable student support system in order not to lose the distance education learner. The Ashland University Instructional Policy for Alternative Instructional Delivery places the successful implementation of the policies with provost's office, which in turn uses the committee to provide advice and oversight for policies and programs outlined in the policy document.

The Ashland University Instructional Policy provides a method for institutions of higher education to design a student support system that will meet the needs of distance education students. The student support system must be problem centered and provide suitable turnaround time for the student learner.

Elon University, in Elon, North Carolina (Anderson, 2001), developed a survival guide for students that includes answers to questions that might be asked when considering Web-based course offerings. The questions (Appendix C) in the Elon University survival guide serve as an excellent marketing and support tool. It is important to ensure that distance education students have the same support systems as would be available for students in the traditional classroom setting.

## CONCLUSION

Faculty member and student support systems must be grounded in an organizational policy that defines the parameters for Web-based and Web-assisted instructional delivery approaches. The policy must provide for technical support and an infrastructure that will allow learning to take place at any time and any place. An extensive amount of planning and coordination by those who are responsible for faculty and student support will be needed. The support systems for faculty members and students must be problem centered and allow for a suitable turnaround time.

## SIGNIFICANT POINTS

- Organizational commitment means developing a policy that ensures that there are adequate funding and support systems in place.
- Professional development and training are key elements of a faculty support system.

- Talk with faculty members who have taught Web-based and Web-assisted courses.
- Students must have excellent writing skills.
- Develop a student support system that is able to meet the expectations and the needs of the students.
- Support systems must be problem centered and allow for suitable turnaround time.
- A student survival guide can act as a screening and marketing tool.

# 4

---

# Transitioning from Classroom-Based Instruction

## BACKGROUND

Moving from face-to-face teaching to a Web-based or Web-assisted instructional learning environment will require the instructor to reevaluate and reconstruct teaching strategies with the responsibility of moving learning from the instructor to the learner. Table 4.1 (Lynch, 1998) illustrates how teaching strategies normally used in the traditional classroom setting can be used in Web-based or Web-assisted courses.

The use of the traditional instruction approaches is easily converted into a Web-based format that lends itself to as much or more interaction between instructor and student. The Web-based format allows for a new lens to be applied to traditional classroom teaching strategies.

Like the instructor, the students also will have to adjust their learning styles to meet the requirements of the Web-based and Web-assisted learning environment. This adjustment means that the instructor must create a learning environment that assists the students in adjusting their learning styles and aids in minimizing student apprehension concerning the use of technology tools and completion of course work.

**Table 4.1.   Transition of Classroom-Based Instruction to the Web**

| Classroom Instruction | Form of Web Instruction | Description of Potential Use |
|---|---|---|
| Class discussions | Chat-synchronous, immediate interactivity | Schedule specific chat times when students may gather to discuss a topic. It is useful to structure the chat by providing questions or topics in advance. |
| Class discussions | Bulletin board–asynchronous, gives time for considered responses | Post questions on the bulletin board and ask for student responses. |
| Role-playing | Multi-user dimensions | Students come to chat in assigned roles; a scenario can be previously posted on a Web page |
| Case studies | Chat | Provide case study in advance (via textbook or Web pages) and ask students to come prepared to chat. |
| Case studies | Bulletin board | Post specific case-related questions to the bulletin board. |
| Case studies | E-mail | Ask for a written analytical assignments to be attached to e-mail. |
| Question and answer sessions | Bulletin board | Designate a topic on the bulletin board for question and answers. |
| Question and answer sessions | Chat | Have chat office hours posted in advance. It is advisable to pick at least two differing times; remember geographical time differences within your student population. |
| Assignments and peer critiques | E-mail attachments | Send attachments to the instructor via e-mail for grading and feedback |
| Assignments and peer critiques | Web page | Post to the Web and send Uniform Resource Locator to the instructor. |
| Assignments and peer critiques | Bulletin board postings | Chat and paste to bulletin board for sharing with the entire class—may also use peer critique with this method. |

*Source:* Lynch, 1998.

## TEACHER-CENTERED VERSUS
## STUDENT-CENTERED CLASSROOMS

After my first year at Ashland University, I came to the realization that I needed to make changes to my instructional delivery approach. I decided to be a risk taker and developed a school finance course in a Web-based format, which has pushed me to develop a school building, grounds, and facilities Web-based course and a Web-assisted school superintendent course. I found that students in the superintendents' licensure program were not interested in busywork but wanted resources that could be used in their present or future job settings.

In the Web-based format I had to restructure my teaching strategies to meet the needs of learners whom I would only periodically see. It meant that I had to move from a teacher-centered to a student-centered approach where the students are empowered to learn independently and, in the case of group study work, be able to teach one another.

Table 4.2 is illustrative of the philosophical changes I needed to make to move from a teacher-centered to student-centered instructional approach. I became a facilitator of information who stresses collaboration, independent student learning, and electronic-centered dialogue between instructor and students. Knowlton (2000) believes that in the student-centered classroom, the professor is not the sole voice of authority or the only one who endowed with knowledge worthy of dissemination. In Knowlton's student-centered classroom, the student takes a more active role in dispensing information, collaborating and interacting with the instructor and students by using a wide range of electronic communication tools.

I have found that teaching Web-based or Web-assisted courses is very time consuming not only in developing the class materials but also in maintaining feedback to students on their assignments and questions. In the Web-based format I meet face to face with students five times, supplemented by chat rooms. The students are connected

**Table 4.2.    A Contrast between the Teacher-Centered
and Student-Centered Classroom**

|  | *Teacher-Centered Classroom* | *Student-Centered Classroom* |
|---|---|---|
| Pedagogical orientation | Positivism. | Constructivism. |
| "Things" | Professor introduces "things" and suggests the implications of those things. | Both professor and students introduce "things," and both offer interpretations and implications. |
| People | Roles of professor and student are regimented: the professor disseminates knowledge, and the student reflects that information. | Roles of professor and student are dynamic: the professor and students are a community of learners. The professor serves as a facilitator and mentor; the students become active participants in learning. |
| Processes | Professor lectures while students take notes. | Professor serves as facilitator while students collaborate with each other and the professor to develop personal understanding of content. |

*Source:* Knowlton, 2000.

with their classmates via e-mail, bulletin board postings, and chatroom discussions. I believe that I have created a class environment that allows for the use of the traditional instructional approaches supplemented by a Web-based and Web-assisted format that provides for as much interaction between students and instructor as would be found in the traditional classroom setting or more. Johnston and Cooley (2001) state, "Student-led inquiry or research asks students to construct significant questions and to design strategies for answering those questions, presenting their findings, and evaluating their products and processes. The processes tend be authentic, requiring higher levels of cognition, and relate both to real life issues and themes across disciplines" (p. 3).

I have used positively the WebCt communication tools in my Web-based and Web-assisted courses. The private e-mail, bulletin board, chat room, and the assignment drop box are excellent vehicles for integrating the interactive dialogue and communication. I believe I have a made a successful transition to an instructional learning environment where the students have become active learners and collaborate positively together in developing responses to case studies and other course assignments.

## STUDENT APPREHENSIONS

In a Web-assisted course, I asked my students what their apprehensions were prior to taking their first Web-based or Web-assisted course. I found that the students were concerned about their ability to complete the coursework, technology malfunctions, appropriate directions to access information, navigating the Web to submit assignments, knowing what to do, being able to get the technology to work, and uncertainty as to what lessons and assignments would be like, type of computer skills needed, and whether or not they would miss the personal contact and networking. One student said, "Not being a huge computer expert, I have learned a lot and can't believe that I have actually been in a chat room and used threaded discussions. I'm using the Web sites more often with improved confidence! Thanks!"

I try to minimize student apprehensions by becoming a facilitator: making learning student-centered, with the students using online study groups, chat rooms, private e-mails, and threaded discussions to do their coursework. I remind students that I am not a technical-oriented person but that I have a created an interactive course environment where they will enjoy learning independence that is often found in the traditional classroom. I stress the need to be patient and not to get frustrated if they have difficulty opening the links or downloading assignments.

## CHANGES TO STUDENT LEARNING STYLES

Like the instructor, students have to change their learning styles when taking a Web-based or Web-assisted course. In a Web-assisted course, I asked the students what changes were made to their learning styles when they took their first Web-based or Web-assisted course. The students said that they had to adjust to more flexibility, organize their time, find course material on the Web, work independently, focus more on reading skills, become more self-motivated, learn to accept the computer and its capability, access a variety of Web sites, and do something different in a nontraditional manner.

The student-centered aspect of my Web-based and Web-assisted courses can be seen in the following student statements: (1) "I learned to like the computer more and appreciate its capability. For my second Web-based class I relaxed more and let the technology do the work. I absolutely loved the chat-room sessions, which were stimulating"; (2) "In the Web-based courses, I found that I was able to access a variety of sites for learning and gained a wealth of knowledge. The Web-based courses enabled me to connect to endless sites. It also enabled me to communicate with the instructor at any hour based on my schedule and receive an answer within a day"; and (3) "I am a self-motivator and I like to have assignments early. I enjoyed the process and learning on the Web. The course was very informative as well as practical and convenient. I would highly recommend a Web-assisted course."

I think it can be seen from the student statements that, as an instructor, I have been able to positively transition from the classroom-based instructional design to a Web-based and Web-assisted instructional design. As an instructor one needs to take into consideration the type of changes in learning styles that my students mentioned so that you can design your course to be nonthreatening and user-friendly.

## CONCLUSION

Using some of the same teaching strategies found in the traditional classroom eases the transition to Web-based and Web-assisted instruction is matter. The traditional classroom instructional strategies of class discussion, role-playing, case studies, question and answer sessions, assignments, and peer critiques can be adapted in Web-based and Web-assisted courses by using chat rooms, bulletin board postings, threaded discussions, Web page postings, assignment links, and e-mails.

The Web-based and Web-assisted instructional environment requires the instructor to become more student-centered and to serve as a coach and mentor whereby the students become active participants in the learning process.

Those students who have not taken Web-based or Web-assisted courses bring apprehensions to the class setting that must be recognized by the instructor. By minimizing student apprehensions and assisting students to adjust their learning styles, you can create a positive alternative instructional learning environment that will meet the expectations and needs of your students.

## SIGNIFICANT POINTS

- The Web-based and Web-assisted instructional learning environment requires the instructor to reevaluate and reconstruct teaching strategies.
- The teaching strategies used in the traditional classroom setting can be used in Web-based and Web-assisted courses.
- The instructor has to adjust teaching strategies and students have to adjust their learning styles.
- The shift from teacher-centered to student-centered instruction allows the instructor to become a facilitator of information who stresses collaboration and independent student learning.

- Technology tools assist in integrating dialogue and communication strategies.
- Understand student apprehensions and know how to assist students to adjust their learning styles.

# 5

# Developing Course Designs That Make Sense

## BACKGROUND

It is most important that Web-based and Web-assisted courses are not overdesigned so that the instructor is unable to deliver the course material and learning outcomes. After teaching several Web-based courses, I had to step back and examine why I was missing the mark in meeting the instructional needs of the students. I discovered that I was not taking the time to design my courses to be user-friendly and I had overestimated the technological capabilities of my students. As I gradually became more comfortable using the technology tools, I was able to design Web-based and Web-assisted courses that met the instructional needs of the students. With each successive on-line course, I have found that the students have become more positive about transitioning to the online course environment.

The course design must be both user-friendly and visually interesting to the students. The instructor needs to find a course delivery environment where the instructor can handle the organization and course design. Our university uses WebCt, where the technology instructional technician works with the instructor in designing a user-friendly online instructional learning environment. The bottom line: Use all available resources to provide the best possible alternative instructional learning environment for your students.

# DESIGN QUESTIONS

In designing Web-based and Web-assisted courses you have to re-think how you would package the course material you have been us-ing in the traditional course setting for the online course setting. Key design questions need to be answered before you start to work on your online course. I found that L. Dee Fink (2003) has a question process that can be used to design either traditional or Web-based and Web-assisted courses. The following is a reflection of how I have applied the questioning process in designing Web-based and Web-assisted courses:

## Initial Phase: Building Strong Primary Components

1. Where are you?
   I was ready for a change in my teaching strategies as I no longer found the traditional classroom setting an exciting learning environment. My teaching strategies were missing the mark. The bottom line is that I needed a change and I was will-ing to be a risk taker, even though I was not a tenured faculty member.
2. Where do you want to go?
   I recognized that Web-based and Web-assisted courses are not appropriate for every student. My changes were designed to meet the needs of the busy, mobile adult learner, and I was looking to find a niche that would provide alternative instruc-tional delivery experiences for adult learners. My challenge was to take the existing course material I was using in my self-contained classroom and reshape it to fit the Web-based and Web-assisted instructional learning format.
3. How do you know if you got there?
   I wanted to make it a priority to stay connected to my students. I was intent on using the WebCt communication tools of e-mails, bulletin board postings, threaded discussions, and chat

rooms. I made it priority to give instant and comprehensive feedback to the student assignments posted in the assignment drop box. My student evaluations improved as I paid more attention to providing timely feedback to student questions and assignments. I would often call the students who were having difficulty using the technology tools or understanding the course assignments, to clarify their questions.

4. How are you going to get there?

At the time I began considering teaching a Web-based course, it was a major risk since I was not a tenured faculty member and there was still some uncertainty about how the university's promotion and tenure committee would view this new type of course delivery. It placed a lot of pressure on me to make sure there was no deviation from the course outcomes and the students' expectations. I decided early on that I was not going to use streaming video, given the potential of computer compatibility problems on the part of the students. In my first Web-based course I converted my traditional course materials into online course modules where the students could access the material through linked resources. The end results have been positive student evaluations with comments about how much they enjoyed the creative course environment.

5. When can copyrighted works be uploaded to or downloaded from the Internet?

I added this question because it is integral to the copyright law as it pertains to the Internet. You are permitted to upload or download copyrighted works when you are the copyright owner of the material, when you have permission from the copyright owner, or when uploading or downloading could be considered fair use. There are copyrighted works, such as Web pages and computer software, that are protected in the same way as works in other media, for example, books and CD/ROMs (Copyright & Ashland University, 2004). The Web site www.benedict.com provides an overview of what the copyright law covers, by major classifications of copyrightable subject matter (Copyright Web site, 2005).

6. Who and what can help?

As I started to examine other online courses and their formats, I found several courses at other institutions of higher education that were similar to the courses that I anticipated teaching. When I was looking to develop my first Web-based course, my university was just starting to examine online courses as an alternative instructional delivery approach. I was fortunate to be named to the university's Alternative Instructional Delivery Committee, which was given the charge of developing policies for online courses. This committee assignment positioned me to work with the instructional technology staff to receive training and design assistance. To keep up to date with the online technology environment, I often attend university professional development sessions where our faculty members present their Web-based or Web-assisted course experiences.

## Intermediate Phase: Assembling the Components into a Dynamic, Coherent Whole

1. What are the major topics in this course?

The first Web-based course I taught was a school finance class based on Ohio's school funding system. The course objectives were as follows:

- To develop an understanding of the economic interests in education, which includes interrelations between and among local governments, school funding decisions, privatization and vouchers, and educational decision making based on pertinent and viable information.
- To develop a familiarity with the school finance system in Ohio: local funding, federal funding, budgetary controls, investments, bonding, borrowing, projections, and bankruptcy.

- To identify strengths and weaknesses of various funding mechanisms and systems.
- To use the Internet to gather school finance data for analysis and research purposes.
- To use case studies and budget analysis as a means of better understanding the complexities of school finance.
- To appreciate the impact of local, state, and federal politics on school finance.
- To learn the art of collaboration and teaming through a variety of online class projects.

As you can see, I fashioned the course objectives to include the course themes and how technology was going to be used to deliver the themes. I spent time with the students reviewing course objectives so that there was a clear understanding that they were going to receive the same material that would be found in the traditional course setting; the only difference is that now it is delivered in an online course environment.

2. What will the students need to do?

So that the students understand the course technology requirements, I have the following statement put in the student's master course schedule:

Each student must have access to a computer which is connected to the Internet. Most of the required readings, as well as other assignments, will be available only through the Internet or the course Web site. You will need to know how to download files such as Adobe.pdf documents and how to print documents from your computer. You will also need a telephone or modem connection speed 56.6 Bauds/Kbs or higher and a web browser (Netscape 4.7 or higher or Internet Explorer 5.0 or higher). Also, you will need to check as to whether or not your computer system has a firewall that would not allow you to use the chat room.

At this point in the design process I add the list of assignments as it pertains to the themes of the course.

3. What is the overall scheme of learning activities?

I laid out the course themes with corresponding assignments in question one. I now organize the course readings for each theme in a Web-based format. Each week there is a course theme with online linked readings, which are sometimes supplemented with printed handouts from the first class.

At this time I also designate which weeks the assignments will be submitted to the assignment drop box. I have made the decision that the assignment drop will be opened for the length of the course and not restricted to a certain date. There are instructors who keep the assignment drop box open only until the day the assignment is due. I found that by not keeping an open assignment drop box, I became overwhelmed with all of the students assignments coming at the same time and my having to try to get back to the students in a timely matter. I have found through the student evaluations that they want immediate feedback.

## Final Phase: Taking Care of Important Details

1. How are you going to grade?

I took the same grading system I used in my traditional courses, which is based on a point total per assignment, and applied that grading system to my Web-based and Web-assisted courses. The WebCt format allows the student to upload a file to the assignment drop box where the instructor can give feedback and assign a point total for the grade.

2. What could go wrong?

Past experience has told me that I need to be prepared to receive feedback from students when they are having difficulty connecting to the WebCt course. Often the student's Web browser is not upgraded or they forget their user name or password. Another problem is that students forget how to use the communication tools or the sequence for uploading their files to the assignment drop box. I remind students that they need to check their chat room to ensure that there is not a firewall that denies the students access to the chat room. I tell the students that they have to be patient when working in the Web-based and Web-assisted instructional learning environment, especially if the university server goes down. In my course outline and during the first class, I tell the students that Microsoft Works is not compatible with WebCt, but invariably there are students who use Microsoft Works and cannot understand why I was unable to read their assignments. The more experience you have in teaching Web-based and Web-assisted courses, the better you will be prepared to anticipate the "bumps in the road."

3. How will students know what you are planning to do?
This is where I now make sure that the course outline and assignment links are finished and can be accessed through the WebCt course design format. I also check each reading link to ascertain as to whether or not they are still linked to an Internet Web site. I test the communication tools both as an instructor and student to ensure that the e-mail system, student course grade card, bulletin board, and chat room are up and running. I will often give prospective students a copy of the course outline and the linked assignments. After consultation with the university instructional technology design technician, the course is ready to be delivered to students in an online format.

4. How will you know how the course is going? How it went?
During the first several weeks of class I will often telephone those students I sense are having difficulty using the WebCt course communication tools. Also, some students have difficulty understanding how to upload their files to the assignment drop box.

I stay connected to the students through the bulletin board postings, threaded discussions, e-mails, and chat room discussions. The WebCt assignment drop box comment feature provides an excellent way for the instructor to give immediate feedback to the students. The students use the same communication tools to communicate with me.

I use the student evaluations and an online technology questionnaire to gather feedback about the curricular and technological aspects of the course. After completing a recent Web-assisted course, the student evaluations revealed that I should move the course to a better instructional space and that I should use more interactive simulations. Because of the students' suggestions, I moved the course to a more user-friendly technology lab and added more simulations to the course-learning activities.

## COURSE DESIGN

I have found that you need to ease into a course design that you feel comfortable using with your students. As you gain experience in teaching Web-based and Web-assisted courses, you can gradually add more bells and whistles. I use the WebCt format, which allows me to provide a course outline that is connected to linked assignments. The linked assignments allow the students to connect to the readings and class assignments. The readings provide the students with the opportunity to expand their resource base.

The use of linked assignments has afforded me the opportunity to provide my students with interactive sites as a part of their class assignments. I have had them do online activities such as a financial peer review of their school district, examination of the fiscal condition of their school district, comparison of a state's local and state school funding system to another state, analysis of their school district's continuous improvement plan and the Seattle Public Schools building budget builder. The use of interactive online learning activities provides the students with hands-on experiences that allow them to better understand the practices and theories of the course. I have received numerous positive student comments about the interactive format of the course and the ability to use the same linked materials in the job setting, especially after the class has been completed.

My instructional design format is fairly straightforward and based on the modules I used in my traditional courses. The following on-line resources provide examples of instructional designs and examples of Web-based and Web-assisted course formats.

### Interactive Instructional Designer

www.merlot.org/artifact/ArtifactDetail.po?oid=1010000000000137945

This site has developed an online tool that asks a series of questions and provides a report that compares your answers to the best research case studies and real-life experiences on building Web-based courses to generate a customized analysis of next steps. The report divides the responses in the categories of Team Information, Course Information, and Student Information; it then delineates your Strengths, Challenges, and Next Steps. Under Next Steps, I was told to do the following: (1) Create a storybook of materials for the course (there is a link that provides examples of how to create storybooks); (2) Develop a syllabus that included concise guidelines about the hardware/software needs, time expectations, and people to contact (there is a link that provides an example of a syllabus statement); (3) Develop a plan for online communication; (4) Since I said that I anticipated starting the course in six months, it was suggested that I start compiling the course materials; and (5) It was suggested that I continue to improve my computer skills. This interactive Web site is an excellent resource for instructors who are interested in designing Web-based and Web-assisted courses (Staub, 2004).

### UMUC—Verizon Virtual Resources Site for Teaching with Technology

www.umuc.edu/virtualteaching/vt_home.html

This site provides examples of resources for appropriate media to accomplish specific learning objectives, research assignments, small group projects, and interactive discussions.

Module One: Using the Web to Design Online Courses assists the instructor in developing and using Web-based media directed at meeting students' learning experiences. Module Two: Delivering Online Interactive Courses assists instructors with perspectives from experienced practitioners as to how to use interactivity as a key influence on students' learning styles.

## Instructional Design Resources

www.ion.uillinois.edu/resources/tutorials/id/index.asp

This site provides a step-by-step process for designing online courses. The subheadings of the major themes in the Web site are linked to descriptions of how to design those areas. The step-by-step process is as follows:

1. Principles of Instructional Design
   a. Instructional design for online courses
   b. Online instruction—important issues to consider
   c. Instructional design worksheet
2. Designing an Effective Course
   a. Designing an exemplary online course
   b. Distribution of content in online courses
   c. Using story boards in online course design
3. Models and Theories
   a. Instructional design models
4. Helping Others Make Their Courses Great
   a. Helping faculty members to create quality online courses
   b. Developing course objectives for chemistry
5. Course Objectives
   a. Developing course objectives
6. Learning Styles
   a. Learning styles and the online course environment

## World Lecture Hall

web.austin.utexas.edu/wlh

The World Lecture Hall contains links to pages created by faculty members worldwide who use the Web to deliver their course materials. It is an excellent resource that provides examples of Web-based and Web-assisted courses.

## ACCOMMODATIONS FOR STUDENTS WITH DISABILITIES

A part of the Web-based and Web-assisted design process is providing accommodations for students with disabilities. At my university the Office of Disability Services assists students with a documented disability that limits one or more life activities, which in the case of Web-based and Web-assisted courses is learning. The students are advised to contact the office before a course starts so that the appropriate academic adjustments can be made to the Web site and Web pages. In a well designed Web-based and Web-assisted course, the student should be able to navigate the Web and course materials notwithstanding the fact that the student may have a disability.

As you design your course it is important that you make contact with the department of information technology to ensure that the Web site and Web pages are accessible for all students, including those with disabilities. The following are examples of evaluation tools that can be used to do an analysis of Web sites and Web pages regarding their accessibility.

- AnyBrowser.com: Tools that can review screen sizes, images replaced by Alternative Text, HTML and link validation, search engine tools, and other browser compatibility tests. (Transformation Tools for Web Content Accessibility, 2005).
- Bobby (www.watchfire.com/resources/bobby-overview.pdf): A Web accessibility desktop that is designed for small Web sites to assist in finding barriers to accessibility. (Transformation Tools for Web Content Accessibility, 2005).

- WebXACT (Webexact.watchfire.com): A free online service where the instructor or the department of informational technology can test single pages of the Web for content quality, accessibility, and privacy issues (Transformation Tools for Web Content Accessibility, 2005).
- A-Prompt (aprompt.snow.utoronto.com): A research project through the University of Toronto where the software is able to examine Web pages for barriers to accessibility and can assist in performing manual and in some cases automatic repairs to Web pages (Academic Community, 2005).

The instructor in a Web-based and Web-assisted instructional learning environment will encounter students that have various kinds of disabilities where the instructional strategies will have to be adjusted to meet the needs of the students. The following are some examples of assistive technologies and adaptive strategies that could be used with students that have disabilities (How People with Disabilities Use the Web, 2005).

Color Blindness

- Web sites that provide sufficient color contrast
- Web sites that provide redundant information for color
- Web sites that provide style sheets that can be turned off with the student's browser or overridden with the student's own style sheet

Low Vision

- Use of large monitors
- Increasing the size of the fonts and images
- Use of screen magnifiers or screen enhancement software
- Selection of typefaces that fit the vision problem
- Combinations of texts and background colors

Blindness

- Screen reader that converts the information to a speech synthesizer or to refreshable Braille for the sense of touch
- Voice browsers
- Text-based browsers
- Braille screen displays and printer output

Hearing Impaired

- Captioning for audio content
- Chat rooms
- Threaded discussions
- E-mails
- Use of supplemental images to highlight content
- Assistive listening devices

Motor Disabilities

- Speech recognition software
- Alternative keyboard—keyboards with extra small or large spacing, keyboards that allow pressing one key at a time, touch screen keyboards, and eye-gaze keyboards
- Specialized mouse
- Layout keys that match the students range of motion
- Head pointer or mouth stick

Dyslexia and Learning Disabilities

- Text to speech software
- Use of captions
- Software that is able to freeze animated graphics
- Reading machine

To actually see the various assistive technology devices for students with disabilities the instructor can go to www.section508.gov/

index.cfm?FuseAction=Content&ID=87 for pictures and explana-
tions. This assistive technology showcase is helpful for the instructor to better understand the type assistive technology devices that are
available to the students. (Academic Community, 2005).

## CONCLUSION

As stated earlier, as an instructor you will have to find your comfort
level with the type of course design you are able to handle and deliver to your students in a user-friendly manner. I found that after
teaching several Web-based and Web-assisted courses that I was beginning to find a balance of the courses being user-friendly and more
visually interesting to the students. It takes time to develop a course
design comfort level for both the instructor and students.

Key design questions need to be answered before an instructor
starts designing a Web-based and Web-assisted course. Under the
three phase design process of Initial Phase: Building Strong Primary
Components; Intermediate Phase: Assembling the Components into
a Dynamic, Coherent Whole; and Final Phase: Taking Care of Important Details, I reflected on my experiences in answering the questions raised about design development. It should be noted that the
design development questions are also applicable to the traditional
course setting. Once you have started teaching Web-based or Web-
assisted courses, it is important to use your student evaluations and
other evaluation instruments to continue to refine your course design
much as you would do when you are teaching in the traditional
course setting.

The instructional design information provided in this chapter is
resource information that can assist you in developing and providing
a user-friendly Web-based and Web-assisted instructional learning
environment for your students. Most importantly you need to find a
comfort level with your course design that is user-friendly for your
students.

## SIGNIFICANT POINTS

- It will take time and patience when developing Web-based and Web-assisted courses.
- The three-phase design and question format is a reflective method of finding the right mix of learning activities that do not overwhelm the instructor and students.
- Check with the copyright owner about uploading or downloading copyrightable works.
- Find your comfort level with the course design that you believe is user-friendly for yourself and your students.
- Web-based and Web-assisted course designs will evolve and change with each course.
- Leverage available course design resources and ideas from practitioners who have developed online courses.
- Rely on your Office of Disabilities Services equivalent to assist you in identifying assistive technology devices.
- Rely on your information technology department to assist you in ensuring that the Web site and Web pages are accessible for all students, including those with disabilities.

# 6

## Interactivity

### BACKGROUND

I recognize that Web-based and Web-assisted instruction courses are not for every student. It has given me the challenge that I needed to add a different perspective to my instructional delivery approaches. I struggled with the question: Could interactivity be achieved in an online course environment?

When I first started using Web-based and Web-assisted instructional approaches my colleagues believed that it would not be as interactive as face-to-face instruction. I made it my mission to make my courses as much as or even more interactive than face-to-face instruction. The obstacle I had to eliminate was the feeling of isolation on the part of the student. My challenge was to use the Web and course technology tools to create an interactive learning environment.

The instructor needs to create a learning environment that allows for the use of traditional instructional approaches supplemented by online instructional strategies that provide for as much or more interaction as would be found in the traditional classroom setting.

## BUMPS IN THE ROAD

As I prepared to do my first Web-based class in the fall of 2000, I started to plan on how I was going to stay connected with my students in a Web-based instructional learning environment. I thought I had a good game plan but soon found out that there were going to be bumps in the road. I have always prided myself to be prepared for any eventuality but the Web-based learning environment was more difficult than I had anticipated.

My game plan was to ensure that the students would leave the first class with a clear understanding of course expectations and acquire the ability to use the WebCt communication tools. What transpired after the first class was confusion on the course expectations and how to use the WebCt technology tools.

During the first class I went through the course outline and the WebCt communication tools. We practiced doing e-mails, bulletin board postings, threaded discussions, opening assignment links, chat room discussions, and assignment drop box activities. I felt good about how the students handled the technology tools and I believed that they were ready to do the online course work. Little did I know what was to happen next.

I left the initial class feeling good about how thorough I had been in preparing the students to navigate the Web-based instructional learning environment. The next day I received phone calls from the majority of my students asking me how they were to connect to WebCt. In my excitement to demonstrate how to use the course technology tools, I had neglected to emphasize that the students first had to go to Ashland University's Web site (www.ashland.edu) and then go to the link that said online classes. Also, I had been rather vague on how the students were to log onto WebCt. After talking some of the students through these procedures, it dawned on me that I had better call the rest of the class to make sure they understood how to access the Ashland University Web site and how to log onto WebCt. In the end, it took a phone call to every student to walk them through connecting to Ashland University's Web site and the login procedures for WebCt.

My next bump in the road occurred when we did our first chat room. The chat room was to be done the third week of the class on a Tuesday at 5:00 P.M. I was excited about using the chat room, which would allow me to connect and interact with the students on a real time basis. As the class time approached, my anxiety level was high. I was excited about using a different medium to interact with my students. When the time came for the class to start, the students began to log in to the chat room and then one by one disappeared because they were having connection difficulties. As this was happening, I received a phone call from one of the students who said that he could not log onto WebCt. I had the student call our technology help desk, and he discovered that his district had a firewall that would not allow him to connect to Ashland University's WebCt program. So the student proceeded to drive home so that he could connect with us.

I received very little meaningful discussion about the class assignments even though I e-mailed the students about them. The discussion was all over the place. The students were discussing everything but the class assignments. Even with my prompts, I had difficulty generating a meaningful discussion. I was relieved when the chat room session ended. I thought to myself that I had failed to provide a meaningful learning experience for my students.

The chat room experience was mortifying to me. And my experiences did not get any better. The next problem occurred with the assignment drop box. I had told the students that this feature would allow them to upload their files and send them to the assignment drop box, which would allow me to grade their assignments and give them instant feedback. Wrong! Some of the students had trouble using the uploading feature and were unable to send me their assignments. I worked with my students over the phone and they were finally able to get the uploading feature to work.

## SMOOTHING OUT THE BUMPS IN THE ROAD

So what went wrong with my first Web-based course? How should I have handled these new interaction activities differently? After finishing my first Web-based course, I decided I needed to carefully review my student evaluations and peer reviews. The student evaluations revealed that the students had not understood the time commitment they had to make to a Web-based course. I found that I needed to do a better job of working with the students to adjust their technology skills to the WebCt course format. I now use an assessment tool as means of analyzing the readiness of each student, which provides me with a means of working closely with those students that need additional technical assistance.

In the Web-based and Web-assisted instructional approaches, I found that the first two weeks of the class are the most critical for students to become accustomed with the online communication tools as the primary source of receiving and sending information. My primary goal in each course is to take the fear out of using the computer and try to create a positive tool that assists in enhancing the student's understanding of the subject matter. I have refined my instructional delivery approaches. If I use a chat room, I post the discussion questions prior to class instead of asking the questions during the online discussions. To personalize the course, I call the students to see how they are doing with their assignments. I have found that e-mails, threaded discussions, and bulletin board postings have become an excellent communication medium.

After the last course session, I use the student evaluations (Appendix D) and the online technology questionnaire (Appendix E) to assist me in finetuning my Web-based and Web-assisted courses. The assessment results have shown that the use of the computer was evenly split between home and work. Several students have indicated it took time to get acquainted with the assignment drop box and the uploading process needed to be explained better by the instructor. The students have liked the use of their private e-mail system for the class and felt that the use of the bulletin board allowed the entire class to view other students' research and was also good for getting updates on class work and related current events. The students have liked the chat room as a means to meet online, with one student commenting, "The only problem might be that the person who can type the fastest wins!"

My student evaluations have improved dramatically since my first Web-based course. The student's comments were that they liked the independence of working online, the timely and thorough instructor's feedback, user-friendly technology tools, flexibility, and having to be self-motivated to complete the course work. Even though the majority of student evaluations have been positive, I continue to refine my teaching strategies in order to minimize the bumps in the road.

## INTERACTION TIPS

As I continue to use Web-based and Web-assisted instructional strategies, it is apparent that there needs to be a high level of instructor-student interaction. It was evident from the bumps in the road that my plan to create an interactive learning environment was well intended but not well organized. I forgot that I needed to provide a mechanism for encouragement so that the students become involved in the Web-based or Web-assisted learning process.

Kearsley (2000) believes that interaction and participation are not the same thing. Participation is involvement and presence without feedback, while interaction is some kind of dialogue between the student and instructor, other students, or the content of the course. In an interactive learning environment, DeNigris and Witchel (2000) believe that, as an instructor, you are not there to judge the student but to assist the student to learn. They believe that you should consider the following ideas as means of creating a positive interactive online learning environment.

- Do encourage participation.
- Do ask meaningful and leading questions.
- Do empathetic listening.
- Do provide feedback, feedback, and more feedback.
- Do not judge.
- Do not ask patronizing questions.
- Do not be overly critical, especially in an open forum where other students may see the criticism.
- Do not send your messages in capital letters, which are perceived as shouting or raising your voice.
- Do not use excessive abbreviations.
- Do not use an excessive amount of humor (pp. 14–17).

These kinds of dos and don'ts are representative examples of how to maintain a positive online interactive learning environment. Table 6.1 (Hanna, et al., 2000) illustrates the types of human interactions and nonhuman interactions that can be used in a Web-based and Web-assisted instructional learning environment.

M. D. Roblyer and Leticia Ekhaml (2000) at westga .edu/~distance/roblyer32.html have designed an instrument that contains a rubric for faculty members to use to determine the degree of interactivity of Web-based and Web-assisted courses. I have used Roblyer's and Ekhaml's instrument to determine my effectiveness in using e-mails, bulletin board postings, threaded discussions, chat rooms, linked assignments, assignment drop box responses, and grade postings. This assessment has assisted me to include learner-to-learner, learner-to-instructor, and instructor-to-learner interactive course activities. I have not tried streaming video, because some of my colleagues have encountered computer compatibility problems. A positive interactive Web-based and Web-assisted learning environment takes planning, time, and encouragement by the instructor. Be a positive and patient facilitator.

**Table 6.1. Types of Interactions**

| Human Interactions | Types of Activities |
| --- | --- |
| Learner-teacher | *Self-regulated learning. (A Web-based conferencing environment may require participants to manage their time, process information, and manage their resources, and evaluate their own work. Learners can seek help when they need it.)<br>*Collaborative problem solving. (As the teacher, you post a problem to be solved by individual learners.)<br>*You and the learners participate in the collective activities and knowledge sharing.<br>*You observe, monitor, and provide feedback to the learners.<br>*You facilitate group processes by responding to questionable situations, such as discussion problems, group dynamics issues, or misunderstandings. |
| Learner-learner | *Learners complete group work to improve their social and critical thinking skills.<br>*Learners access group knowledge and support through collaborative problem solving.<br>*Learners design a Web site for an instructional program. |
| Learner-guest expert or Learner-community member | *Learners collaborate with guests on projects to gain diverse expertise.<br>*Learners discuss real-life situations with practitioners in the community.<br>*Learners work together with community members to solve problems and share knowledge. |
| Learner-tools | *Learners operate software (text copying and pasting, file transferring, image grabbing, brainstorming, outlining, and flow charting).<br>*Learners manipulate software (changing contents, values, and/or parameters to verify, test, and extend understanding).<br>*Learners communicate using the software (promoting discourse, sharing ideas, reviewing work, asking questions, and collaborating). |
| Learner-content | *Learners work with and make sense of the information available on the Web, in books, and in databases. |
| Learner-environment | *Learners work with resources and simulations (Web-based searches, image libraries, source documents, and online databases). |

*Source:* Hanna, D.E., Glowacki-Dulka, M., & Conceição, 2000.

## INTERACTIVE LEARNING ACTIVITIES

My classes are structured to include handouts and online-linked materials. I have been able to structure an interactive Web-based and Web-assisted instructional environment. As a part of the instructional learning environment, I have used such activities as school district financial peer reviews, state school finance reform comparisons, state school finance litigation comparisons, online school district budget building activities, Ohio School Facilities Commission's square footage program of requirement calculation CD/ROM, and a school district five-year enrollment forecast (floppy disk). In an October 15, 2000, peer review the evaluator states, "The class used the Seattle City School District Budget builder program to study the school building budgeting process. It was interesting to see a totally different technique being used." The peer review of October 17, 2002, speaks positively to in-class Web-based interactivity that included the five-year enrollment forecast instrument and the Ohio School Facilities CD/ROM building program square footage calculation. These types of interactive learning activities provide the students with in-class and online hands-on experiences that allow them to better understand the best practices and theories through the Web-based and Web-assisted course delivery approach.

I found through my student evaluations and the technology course assessment tool that I have hit on a course design that works for the graduate students in my courses. I have found that my confidence level has been reinforced when the students' feedback is positive about the course. It is all about finding your niche and what works best for you as an instructor. Above all, be patient and be able to adapt to situations, especially in the Web-based or Web-assisted learning environment.

## CONCLUSION

There will always be bumps in the road that the instructor will have to overcome to succeed in the Web-based and Web-assisted learning environment. Creating an interactive Web-based and Web-assisted course does not happen overnight. It takes a game plan, which requires thorough planning and preparation by the instructor. It is up to the instructor to ensure that the students are capable and ready to handle course expectations and technology tools. The course should be designed to include learner-to-learner, learner-to-instructor, and instructor-to-learner interactive course activities. The instructor should encourage the students to learn and also take a proactive role with them to ensure that they succeed in the Web-based and Web-assisted learning environment. The integration of human interactions and nonhuman interactions assist to balance the type of activity students will encounter during the course.

Their use of preliminary student readiness assessment tools, student evaluations, peer reviews, and technology course assessment tools are excellent instruments to assist the instructor to redesign his or her Web-based and Web-assisted courses. For me, these kinds of evaluation instruments have assisted in developing Web-based and Web-assisted courses that are positively accepted by my students. It is all about finding a niche and what works best for you.

## SIGNIFICANT POINTS

- There will be bumps in the road.
- Be prepared to adjust to a new instructional learning environment.
- Consider using learner-to-learner, learner-to-instructor, and instructor-to-learner interactive activities.
- Balance human and nonhuman interactions.
- Provide positive feedback to students. Do not be a judge!
- Be patient and flexible and become a positive facilitator of information and knowledge.
- Use encouragement to create a positive interactive learning environment.
- Use evaluation instruments to assist in redesigning your course.
- Find your niche and do what works best for you.

# 7

# Feedback

## BACKGROUND

In Web-based and Web-assisted courses, instructor and student feedback are integral elements to designing and maintaining a viable instructional learning environment. The transition from face-to-face instruction to Web-based and Web-assisted instruction requires rethinking how you, as an instructor, are going to stay connected with your students.

The challenge is to maintain a balance between your institutional responsibilities and the ability to adjust your instructional strategies to provide adequate communication and feedback to your students. In my early Web-based and Web-assisted courses, I received complaints from the students about my lack of communication and feedback relative to course assignments and student questions. I discovered that I needed to develop a continuous feedback system that keeps students informed about their progress and achievement. Equally important was developing a way for students to stay connected to the instructor and classmates. I needed to develop an online instructional environment that emphasized collegiality and openness.

Palloff and Pratt (2005) believe that the following guidelines are applicable for effective feedback by the instructor with students and also for students to use when providing feedback to the instructor and classmates.

- Don't just make up feedback as you go along. Plan ahead.
- Before you start to type, think first about what you want to say. Get your ideas straight in your head, and figure out how they all fit together.
- Use short paragraphs. This forces you to express yourself with a minimum number of words.
- When you write something, make sure people understand you. Read the message out loud before you send it.
- If you are quoting a message, keep it brief so that people do not have to scroll all the way through the message looking for the part that you wrote.
- Simply saying that you agree with something does not add much to the conversation. State some of the reasons why you agree so you will look like a person who thinks carefully and considers all the facts.
- Make sure your message is worded professionally and not harshly to avoid insulting those who will read it (p. 49).

It is important for the instructor in the Web-based and Web-assisted instructional learning environment to provide opportunities for instructor and student feedback. Without a dual feedback system in place, the instructor has limited the potential of the Web to provide a dynamic and flexible learning environment.

## INSTRUCTOR FEEDBACK

The success of Web-based and Web-assisted courses is based on the instructor's ability to develop a feedback system that will meet the concerns and needs of the students. In the Jupiter Communications Study, there are several items that emerged about students' attitudes toward online learning that the instructor should anticipate and address through technical assistance, communication, and feedback strategies. These items are: (1) Variation in computer access can result in attitudinal differences; (2) Experience in the use of computers in distance education courses versus traditional classrooms and home settings can also affect students' perceptions; (3) A wide variety of achievement levels and attitudes exist among both online and traditional learners; and (4) The lack of training in computers is the strongest inhibitor to successfully completing an online course (Peters, 2001). It is imperative that the instructor design a communication and feedback system that addresses the perceptions and attitudes of students taking Web-based and Web-assisted courses. A viable communication and feedback system will meet student attitudinal needs and eliminate student confusion and frustrations during the course.

Effective procedures for instructor feedback are the most important features of successful online courses. Students who have a comfort level with the traditional classroom setting seem to expect more traditional feedback and are frustrated if they do not receive the level of attention they expect (Coomey & Stephenson, 2002).

## INFORMATION AND ACKNOWLEDGMENT FEEDBACK

Information feedback provides communication, such as an answer to a question or assigning a grade accompanied with instructor comments (Graham et al., 2001). This kind of feedback needs to be continual throughout the course. I begin the semester by providing information to students through e-mails and bulletin board postings, but I fall into the trap of becoming inconsistent as the course progresses. I have been negligent in giving feedback on a threaded discussion that has already occurred. Therefore, I restructured my time to make sure that I provide timely feedback on threaded discussions and bulletin postings pertaining to class assignments. I have found general bulletin postings and open threaded discussions to be the most effective means of providing course information to my students. I can confine my feedback to the class as a whole and not be overwhelmed by trying to respond to individual students.

The WebCt course format provides a student an informational base that consists of a course calendar, course syllabus, assignment drop box, grade book, e-mail, chat room, and bulletin board.

The following is an example of information feedback from me to a student who had submitted his school board president interview assignment that was required for my Web-assisted superintendent course:

Jack:

Thanks for another good review. This is the first comment that I have received where the board member is concerned about the importance of the working relationship between the superintendent and treasurer. If there are not open lines of communication, life in the superintendent's office can be very uncomfortable.

School finance is always going to be with us. The trust building by the board and superintendent with community needs to be ongoing. Misunderstanding leads to public unrest.

The board member's concern for academic progress is a good thing. The district goals should be directed at showing gains in the areas identified by the board. Fiscal resource is the wild card.

Positive communication is central to staying connected to the community and maintaining a positive working relationship with the superintendent. The lack of positive communications will lead to ineffective district leadership on the part of the board and superintendent.

I think all of the superintendents' candidacy questions were excellent because they focused on the leadership strengths of the candidate. The board needs to know upfront whether or not there is a fit with the board and community. Good questions to also ask when doing reference checks.

It certainly appears you have a knowledgeable board president.

Keep up the good work!

Jim Van Keuren

What I tried to do with my informational feedback was to let the student know that I have appreciated his past work. I gave the student a concise analysis of this board president interview writeup and

I concluded with positive reinforcement about the course work that the student has done online.

I make an extra effort to praise the students even if there is some corrective action that needs to be done to their assignment. I have found in the Web-based and Web-assisted instructional learning environment that it is easier to give individual student praise than in the traditional classroom setting.

Acknowledgment feedback confirms that an event has occurred, such as the instructor sending an e-mail confirming that a question or assignment has been submitted and that a response is forthcoming. This kind of feedback can take a lot of time and effort. In the face-to-face instructional learning environment the instructor is able to respond instantly and give further explanation if there is a need.

I pride myself on quick responses to students' questions. The following is an example of acknowledgment feedback from my Web-assisted superintendent course where I responded within an hour of the student's e-mail.

Good morning Dr. Van Keuren:
 I have tried several times this week to connect to the assignment page. However, for some reason I am not able to connect. There seems to be no problem with the other connections. Please advise. It might be my computer connection. Please check the connection for me.
 Thank you. Susan.

Susan:
 I used your username and password and was able to open the assignment page. Try it again. If you still are having difficulty, we might be able to use a computer at the educational service center tomorrow night.
 Jim Van Keuren

In the acknowledgment feedback, I responded as soon as possible to let the student know that I was able to open the assignment page from my computer. Since the class was meeting the next evening, I gave the student the opportunity to work with me to see if we could solve her problem. It should be noted that the student found prior to our class that she was following the wrong sequence to open the assignment page.

It is important that the instructor develops viable information and acknowledgment feedback systems that give prompt responses to student assignments and questions. These two types of feedback systems, if used correctly, can be as or more effective than what is done in the traditional classroom setting.

## EVALUATIVE FEEDBACK

I use a preliminary assessment tool (Appendix A) to ascertain the student's technology skills and comfort level with taking an online course, and I use the student evaluations (Appendix D) and online technology questionnaire (Appendix E) at the end of each course to gather feedback regarding my instructional abilities and about the technology aspects of the course. I feel that it is important to obtain the student evaluative feedback to know what changes I might make to the course. Also, as an instructor, I want to know whether or not the students encountered any confusion and frustration during the course.

The success of my Web-based courses has been premised on the student's ability to access the assignment links and to turn in the homework, which is dependent on the type of Web browser they use. The feedback from the online technology questionnaire has indicated that some students had computer freeze-up problems with certain Internet services and other students had crashing problems when trying to download materials from the links. A few of the students during my first few classes indicated that some of the posted assignments on the bulletin board were inaccessible because they were done in a WordPerfect format. Students have said that at times the assignment drop box took time getting used to but in the end became a positive part of the class. The students have said that they like the use of their own class e-mail system and felt that the use of the bulletin board was a feature that allowed the entire class to view other students' research. Also it was good for getting updates on class work and related current events. The students liked the use of the chat room as a means of conversing on a real time basis.

The student evaluations and the online technology questionnaire have directed me to move from three face-to-face meetings to a fourth meeting with an optional meeting for technology training. I have made a concentrated effort to personally contact the students through more phone calls, e-mails, bulleting board postings, and increased chat room sessions. I view my enhanced communication efforts as a means of keeping the students accountable for meeting and understanding the course requirements. The additional contact time has allowed me to assist students with their initial technology problems such as connecting to the Internet, eliminating firewalls to the chat room, and determining how to use the assignment drop box.

I have found that the first two weeks of class are the most critical for students to become accustomed to the online communication tools as the primary source of sending and receiving information. My goal in each course is to take the fear out of using the computer and to ensure that the computer becomes a positive tool that assists in enhancing the students' understanding of the subject area.

There are free resources on the Web available to instructors to assist in developing feedback systems in their courses. They can be found at www.freedback.com and www.response-o-matic.com (Hazari & Schnorr, 1999). The more opportunities for student-to-student, instructor-to-student, and student-to-instructor feedback, the better the ability to provide an interactive instructional learning environment.

## CONCLUSION

The transition to the Web-based and Web-assisted course setting requires the instructor to develop dynamic student-to-student, instructor-to-student, and student-to-instructor feedback systems. I discovered that I needed to develop a continuous feedback system to students regarding their progress and achievement.

Pallof and Pratt (2005) guidelines provided an organized approach for instructor and student feedback systems. Information and acknowledgment feedback provide for a system of prompt answers to assignments and student questions.

Instructor feedback is the key to meeting the concerns and needs in a Web-based and Web-assisted instructional learning environment. Student attitudes toward online learning must be addressed through technical assistance, communication, and feedback strategies. The instructor must be able to design a communication and feedback system that addresses the perception and attitudes of students taking Web-based and Web-assisted courses.

The preliminary online assessment tool provides the instructor with information on how students might handle a Web-based learning environment. The use of student evaluations and the online technology questionnaire are excellent instruments to gather feedback about the instructor's instructional capabilities and the technology aspects of the course. There are other feedback instruments on the Web that can be tailored to meet the instructor's feedback and communication needs. Continual student-to-student, instructor-to-student, and student-to-instructor feedback is needed for Web-based and Web-assisted courses to succeed.

## SIGNIFICANT POINTS

- The transition from the traditional classroom to Web-based and Web-assisted instructional learning environment requires feedback systems that meet the response and instructional needs of both the instructor and students.
- An effective feedback system is one that allows students to stay connected to the instructor and classmates.

- Organize messaging techniques so that they are timely, concise, and positive.
- Information and acknowledgment feedback systems provide prompt answers to assignments and student questions.
- The instructor's feedback system should address the perceptions and attitudes of students taking Web-based and Web-assisted courses.
- Feedback instruments assist in developing positive student-to-student, instructor-to student, and student-to-instructor feedback.

# 8

# Don't Drop the Ball!

## BACKGROUND

The challenge in teaching a Web-based or Web-assisted course is to provide a design that has academic rigor and contains the learning outcomes of the course syllabus. Some of your colleagues probably believe that Web-based and Web-assisted courses have watered down subject matter and are lacking in accountability because the instructor and students are not meeting the face-to-face (in person) clock hour requirements. For these reasons it is important that you don't drop the ball.

Kearsley (2000) comments, "Some excellent teachers who enjoy classroom presentations and in-person contact with students do not find the online environment as rewarding or comfortable to teach in" (p. 88). This is the crux of the matter for the instructor who has been teaching in the traditional classroom setting and is now considering a move to Web-based or Web-assisted courses.

At the heart of creating a viable instructional learning environment in a Web-based or Web-assisted course is how the instructor is going to meet the learning outcomes of the course and develop positive instructor-to-student, student-to-student, and student-to-instructor interactions and relationships.

## WHAT HAVE WE LEARNED?

The moving to the Web-based instructional learning environment is a paradigm shift for using technology as an alternative instructional delivery tool. It is a major change in how the content is delivered and you must ensure that there is the same kind of academic rigor found in most face-to-face instructional settings.

What I look for in my student evaluations is their reaction to how I delivered the course materials, my accessibility, responses to their questions and concerns, whether or not the course expectations were clear, and suggestions on how I can improve the course. I use student evaluations to determine what degree I gained the student's respect and trust. It is important that you spend time reviewing with your students the course expectations, software and hardware needs, how to use the technology tools, and the time commitment needed to complete the course work. The last thing you want to happen is a dysfunctional course learning environment where the course expectations are not clear and where the students and instructor are not aligned as to the learning outcomes of the course. You must be able to provide your students with the opportunity to contact you at any time and any place. Immediate feedback to students concerns and questions are essential in this new course environment.

The kind of support system your institution of higher education has in place is crucial to succeed in this alternative instructional learning environment. You need to talk with the instructional technology staff and your fellow colleagues to ascertain the depth and breadth of the faculty and student support systems that are available for Web-based and Web-assisted courses. You need to determine if there is provision for professional development and what resources are available to support your course design work. Most importantly, your institution's support system must be problem centered and needs to allow for a prompt turnaround time to meet instructor and student needs.

As I contemplated transitioning from the classroom-based to the Web-based and Web-assisted instructional learning environment, I thought about winning student respect and trust and to ensure that there were adequate support systems in place. As I reevaluated my instructional strategies, I found that the majority of the strategies I used in the traditional courses could be refined and used in Web-based and Web-assisted courses. This meant that I needed to take into consideration the students' course apprehensions and focus my new instructional strategies to assist my students in adjusting their learning styles. I have now become a facilitator of information who stresses collaboration and independent student learning by using the course technology tools to integrate dialogue and communication strategies.

I found that it is important to design Web-based and Web-assisted courses that are user-friendly and visually interesting to the students. An overdesigned course could lead to inability by the instructor to deliver course materials and learning outcomes. As a course designer you need to take time and be patient in designing your courses. You need to find a comfort level with a course design that you believe, as an instructor, you and your students will be able to successfully handle. Reviewing a three-phased approach of Initial Phase: Building Strong Primary Components; Intermediate Phase: Assembling the Components into a Dynamic, Coherent Whole; and the Final Phase: Taking Care of Important Details can assist you in designing your courses. Do not be afraid to leverage course design resources and ideas from practitioners who have developed Web-based and Web-assisted courses.

There will be bumps in the road where you will have to adjust your course design and instructional strategies. It is important to create a leaning environment that balances the human and nonhuman interactions through the use of instructor-to-student, student-to-student, and student-to-instructor interactive activities. As an instructor you need to become a facilitator of information and knowledge and use continual encouragement to create a positive interactive learning environment. The use of student evaluations and technology questionnaires will assist you in finding your niche and what works best for you.

I found that I needed to adjust my instructional delivery strategies and include a feedback system that is responsive to student questions and instructional needs. The instructor must be able to design an information and acknowledgment feedback system that addresses the perception and attitudes of the students and at the same time provides positive student-to-student, instructor-to-student, and student-to-instructor interactions.

## CONCLUSION

Coomey and Stephenson (2002) state, "The challenges for education arise from the changes in working life and society, and these changes should be reflected in teaching as well. Virtual classrooms, electronic chat rooms, and bulletin boards are just sophisticated tools that teachers can use in creating the best possible opportunities for students to learn. What the teacher knows about learning, and the relationship he or she develops with the students, remain just as essential in virtual classrooms as in physical classrooms" (p. 148).

If you are considering teaching Web-based or Web-assisted courses, the pressure is on you not to drop the ball but to use what you know about learning and interacting with students to create a dynamic instructional learning environment.

## SIGNIFICANT POINTS

- Teaching Web-based and Web-assisted courses is not for every instructor.
- Teaching Web-based and Web-assisted courses is a paradigm shift in how we use technology as an alternative instructional delivery tool.

- Winning student respect and trust in Web-based and Web-assisted courses are key to maintaining a functional learning environment where the instructor and students are aligned as to the learning outcomes.
- The institution's support systems need to be problem centered and allow for a suitable turnaround time to meet instructor and student needs.
- Transitioning from the classroom-based to the Web-based or Web-assisted instructional learning environment means you will need to shift your instructional strategies to become more student centered.
- Developing a course design comfort level for instructor and students takes time and patience. Don't be afraid to leverage course design features from outside sources.
- Balance human and nonhuman interactions.
- Develop an information and acknowledgment feedback system that provides timely responses to student assignments and questions.
- The feedback system should take into consideration the perceptions and attitudes of the students.
- Don't drop the ball; use what you know about learning and interacting with students.

# Appendix A

## Self-Evaluation for Potential Online Students

**W**ill online learning fit your circumstances, lifestyle, and educational needs? Here are some basic questions to ask yourself in deciding if an online program is right for you. You must have Javascript enabled for this quiz to work. Your evaluation will be given in a pop-up window.

1. Do you have (or are you willing to obtain) access to a computer and phone line at home?
   O Yes
   O No
2. Do you feel that high quality learning can take place without face-to-face interaction?
   O Yes
   O No
3. Can you dedicate 4 to 6 hours a week (anytime during the day or night) to participate in the learning process?
   O Yes
   O No
4. Are you a self-motivated and self-disciplined person?
   O Yes
   O No

5. When it comes to schoolwork and deadlines, are you a pro-crastinator?
   - O Yes
   - O No

6. Are you comfortable communicating in writing?
   - O Yes
   - O No

7. Do you enjoy reading?
   - O Yes
   - O No

8. Are class discussions helpful to you?
   - O Yes
   - O No

9. Do you subscribe to the value of introducing critical thinking into the learning process?
   - O Yes
   - O No

10. Do you think increased learning will take place through sharing your work, life, and educational experiences as part of the learning process?
    - O Yes
    - O No

11. Are you comfortable with e-mail, computers, and new technologies?
    - O Yes
    - O No

12. Does your lifestyle (family, work, or personal schedule) make it difficult for you to attend courses during the day?
    - O Yes
    - O No

# Appendix B

## Ashland University Institutional Policy for Alternative Instructional Delivery

Consistent with its stated mission, "to serve the educational needs of all students, undergraduate and graduate, traditional and non-traditional, full and part time," Ashland University wishes to provide opportunities for students whose circumstances make it difficult or impossible to achieve their educational objectives by enrolling in traditionally scheduled classes. To provide these persons a greater measure of access and convenience to courses and programs while maintaining a high standard of instructional quality, Ashland University intends to offer classes in a variety of time-and-place-shifted formats. In particular, it is the intent of this policy to encourage offering classes that will enable students to complete a program or meet an educational objective. By adopting and implementing this policy, Ashland University hopes to extend its academic programming to populations of students not now fully served.

This policy is intended to provide opportunities primarily for students who cannot or prefer not to enroll in Ashland University's traditionally scheduled classes. Courses and programs offered under the provisions of this policy are, therefore, not designed or intended to compete with or diminish the experience of traditionally enrolled students taking classes on campus.

*Definitions*

*Alternative Instructional Delivery.* Alternative Instructional Delivery refers to offering classes in ways that do not require the physical presence of the learner and instructor in the same space at the same time to carry out the instructional process. Alternative instructional delivery typically employs some technology or combination of technologies.

1. The two principal modes of alternative instructional delivery are Web-based courses and interactive video.

*Web-based courses.* Web-based courses are courses in which most instruction in the class (>70%) is carried out using Web-based materials and interaction.

*Interactive Video.* Interactive Video courses are courses in which an instructor live at a point of origination carries out instruction with students present at one or more distant sites by means of interactive audio and video technology.

2. Web-assisted courses and Web-enhanced courses, while employing some of the technology, are not included in this document as alternative instructional delivery.

*Web-assisted courses.* Web-assisted courses are courses in which a substantial part of instruction (30-70%) is carried out using Web-based materials and interaction.

*Web-enhanced courses.* Web-enhanced courses are courses in which a part of a class (<30%) is carried out using Web-based materials and interaction.

In addition to these primary formats, alternative instructional delivery may include the use of instructional material in a variety of forms and media to enable students to take classes in a time or place-shifted mode.

*Stipulations*

In developing and implementing a program of alternative instructional delivery, we proceed from the following stipulations:

1. The policy and program shall focus on and encourage alternative instructional delivery for programs designed to meet a degree, licensure, certificate, or other educational goal.
2. Courses developed under this policy shall meet the same expectations for rigor and quality of instruction as their regularly scheduled counterparts on campus.
3. Courses offered under this policy shall regularly be assessed both by students and by the department and faculty offering them to determine effectiveness.
4. Courses offered under this policy shall be fiscally self-supporting.
5. Faculty and departments offering courses under this policy shall be encouraged, supported, and rewarded for their support.
6. Departmental faculty and academic departments shall be the primary decision makers in determining whether to offer any courses(s) in one of these formats.
7. Students enrolled in courses offered by alternative instructional delivery shall have access to the same essential university services as their residential counterparts.
8. Except as required by external accredited agencies or other review bodies, Ashland University shall make no distinction between sections or instances of courses taken in an alternative instructional delivery format and those taken in a traditional format.

With the above understanding and stipulations, courses may be developed and offered in alternative instructional delivery formats under the provisions and specifications set forth below.

I. Developing and offering AID courses
  A. General Considerations
    1. General Considerations
      Courses selected to be developed for Web-based distance or other time and place shifted modes of instructional delivery must already be included in the regular undergraduate or graduate catalog at Ashland University.

   2. Course selection

Courses selected to be developed for alternative instructional delivery must be approved by the appropriate department chair and academic dean.

B. Specific Delivery Formats

   1. Web-Based Format

      a.) Training

Faculty intending to teach Web-based distance courses will complete twelve hours of training or demonstrate equivalent competency at Information Technology's Instructional Support Lab before or during the development of their first Web-based course.

      b.) Payment

(1) Faculty will receive three hours of teaching credit (in load or a Supplemental Contract paid at the regular undergraduate payment schedule, receiving half of the supplemental at the beginning and the remainder once the course has been completed), and a $500 course development grant for initial development of Web-based delivery of the course.

(2) Faculty may apply for a New Dimensions Grant to support course maintenance and revision.

(3) Faculty teaching students via Web-based instruction are paid at the rate indicated in the most recent *Supplemental Contract Schedule* under the column for alternative instructional delivery.

      c.) Course Material

(1) All course materials shall be considered works for hire in which Ashland University will grant faculty members an exclusive license to the material.

(2) The exclusive license will require the faculty member's approval for all subsequent use of the course except for promotional and public relations purposes by the university. All other use of course material must be authorized by the faculty member.

(3) It is a breach of this policy for a faculty member to offer instruction for pay outside the university using Web-based material developed under the previsions of this policy without the approval of their academic dean.

(4) The shelf life of course materials is considered to be two years. Each course offered for Web-based distance instructional delivery shall be reviewed following procedures established within each department for accuracy and quality of content every two years. Course materials will be withdrawn if:

a) they are determined to be inaccurate, incomplete or out of date.

b) the faculty member requests their removal.

c) the faculty member is no longer employed by Ashland University.

d) the same course is redeveloped.

(5) Options available to faculty who leave the university at the conclusion of an academic term:

a) withdraw the course materials.

b) seek adjunct status to continue to offer the course.

c) permit continued use of the course materials by Ashland University.

(6) When a faculty member leaves the university during the term a course is offered, the university is entitled to use the course materials to the conclusion of that term.

d) Undergraduate Review

(1) Undergraduate courses offered by alternative instructional delivery, after their initial offering, shall be subject to review by the Faculty Senate to determine the fidelity of the class to the approved master syllabus.

(2) In the case of undergraduate course offerings found to depart substantially from the master syllabus,

the Faculty Senate may request suspension of further offerings of that course until steps have been taken to bring the course into conformity with the master syllabus.

(3) No undergraduate course intended to count for CORE credit may be offered without the approval of the CORE Advisory Committee.

e) Graduate Review

(1) Graduate courses offered by alternative instructional delivery, after their initial offering, shall be subject to review by the Graduate Council to determine the fidelity of the class to the approved master syllabus.

(2) In the case of graduate course offerings found to depart substantially from the master syllabus, the Graduate Council may request suspension of further offerings of that course until steps have been taken to bring the course into conformity with the master syllabus.

f) Department Revenue Share

The academic department originating the course offering will receive $100 for each offering of a section, plus $5 per student enrolled.

g) Class Size

The normal section size for web-based distance instructional delivery sections is twenty students, with a minimum of eight students per section and a maximum of twenty-five. With the permission of the department chair and instructor, the enrollment in a section may be increased to a maximum of thirty students. When fewer than eight students wish to enroll for Web-based instruction in a class, they will register for individual Web-based instruction (section 1.10). The instructor will be paid under the provisions of the most recent *Supplemental Contract Schedule* under the column for alternative instructional delivery.

h)  Individual Web-Based Instruction
With the approval of the faculty member, department chair, dean, and program director, a student may enroll in a course for which Web-based instruction is available. A maximum of seven students may enroll for any single course under this arrangement.

i)  Class Meetings
Web-based distance courses, including Individual Web-Based Instruction, at Ashland University shall include a minimum of two face-to-face contact sessions with students, unless arrangements are made in advance for proxy meeting at an approved location.

j)  Tuition
Web-based distance courses, including Individual Web-Based Instruction, may not be taken as part of the comprehensive tuition rate. All Web-based distance undergraduate course offerings are billed at the evening/weekend tuition and fee schedule.

2.  Interactive Video Format

a)  Training
Faculty intending to teach interactive video courses will complete one (1) hour of training or demonstrate equivalent competency at Information Technology's Instructional Support Lab before or during the development of their first interactive video course.

b)  Payment to Faculty
Faculty will receive a $200 course development grant for initial development of each interactive video course. After the first offering of a given course, faculty will receive a $100 grant for each subsequent offering of that interactive video course.

c)  Course Material Ownership
All interactive video course materials shall be considered works for hire in which Ashland University will grant faculty members an exclusive license to the material.

The exclusive license will require the faculty member's approval for all subsequent use of the course materials for promotional and public relations purposes by the university. All other use of course material must be authorized by the faculty member.

d) The normal aggregate size for an interactive video course (total enrollment of source and remote sites) is twenty-five (25) students, with an aggregate minimum of twelve (12) students. With the permission of the department chair and instructor, the enrollment may be increased to a maximum of thirty (30) students. Remote sites shall enroll a minimum of three (3) students to enable a course to be offered at that site. With the permission of the department chair and instructor, a remote site may enroll less than three. No single course offering shall go to more than three distant sites.

e) Class Meetings
   Interactive video courses are synchronous, shifting place of meeting, but not time. Instructors are encouraged to visit each remote site twice during a course, transmitting that class session from the given remote site.

f) Tuition
   Interactive video courses may not be taken as part of the comprehensive tuition rate. All interactive video undergraduate course offerings are billed at the applicable regular tuition and fee rate.

II. Administration of Alternative Instructional Delivery

   A. Alternative Instructional Delivery at Ashland University shall be administered under the auspices of the Provost's Office.

   B. The University Alternative Instructional Delivery Coordinating Committee shall have overall responsibility for supporting the vision and encouraging development of alternative instructional delivery at Ashland University.

C. The Committee reports to the Provost and provides advice and oversight for the policy and program outlined in this document.

D. Membership on the Committee is through appointment by the Provost for renewable, three-year terms. Terms shall be staggered to provide continuity.

E. The Committee shall work in close cooperation with the Executive Director for Information Technology in developing alternative instructional delivery resources and programs.

F. The Committee shall work in close cooperation with Executive Director for Information Technology in developing alternative instructional delivery resources and programs.

C:\My Files\John Bee\Web-based Distance Instruction Policy\ 02-12-02. wor

Revised:

Developing and offering AID courses, B, 1, b (Academic council 7-14-04)

# Appendix C

## Elon University Survival Guide
## Questions for Web-Based Courses

### GENERAL

- What is a Web-based course?
- Why is Elon offering the Web-based course?
- What courses are offered?
- Why should I consider taking a Web-based course?
- Who is eligible to take a Web-based course?
- Can I take both an on-campus course and a Web-based course?
- Can I take a Web-based course and live on campus?
- Do I get the same credit as an in-class course?
- What about transfer credit for Web-based courses?
- Isn't a course taught in a classroom better?

### FEES AND FINANCES

- What are the costs for Web-based courses?
- What are the hidden costs?
- Will my financial aid still apply?
- What is the refund policy with Web-based courses?

## WHAT IS REQUIRED?

- Do I need any special computer skills to take a Web-based course?
- What are the computer hardware and software requirements to take a Web-based course?

## LOGISTICS

- How do I register for a Web-based course?
- Will I have to come to campus during the course?
- When can I begin the course?
- How long do I have to complete the course?
- How do I get a textbook or other supplementary materials?
- How are the tests and exams given?
- How are the assignments turned in?
- Will the course be available day or night?
- What if I cannot access the course server?
- How can I contact the professor?
- Will I be given more time to complete the course if I have a hardware or software problem?
- How do I get my grades?
- If I need help, how do I get in touch with campus services?

## WORKLOAD

- How much work will the course require?

## WHAT TO DO IF YOU ARE INTERESTED

- Where do I begin?
- How can I learn more about Web-based courses?
- What if I register for a Web-based course but can't attend the orientation session?

# Appendix D

## Student Evaluation Instrument

### ASHLAND UNIVERSITY DEPARTMENT OF GRADUATE EDUCATION

Student Feedback to Instructor—Revised September 2002

*Ashland University believes student evaluation to be an important component for faculty reflection on their teaching. This form provides valuable information for faculty to self-assess performance and to improve teaching. This evaluation form deserves your careful attention and full consideration.*

Select a strength of response and mark on the accompanying Scantron Form.

**DO NOT write on this form.**

a    b    c    d    e

**STRONGLY AGREE**             **STRONGLY DISAGREE**

1. The instructor established a climate that encouraged me to learn.
2. I felt free to clarify points and express my opinions.
3. I was encouraged to explore a range of ideas.
4. The instructor helped me understand the content of the course.
5. The expectations of the course were clear to me as the course progressed.
6. The instruction prepared me to meet the course expectations.
7. The instructor provided feedback to support my learning.

8. The instructor provided instructional support and course materials where appropriate. (Examples include textbooks, readings, research, and technology.)
9. Course experiences (examples include readings, papers, projects, labs, lectures/presentations, and field experiences) were appropriate to the expectations of the course.
10. The assessment methods were appropriate for the expectations of the course.
11. The instructor was knowledgeable about the content.
12. The instructor was interested in the content.
13. The instructor was available in person, by phone, or e-mail if I needed help.

Please answer the following in writing on the Scantron Form comment area. Please print clearly.
What aspects did you like about this course?
What suggestions do you have for improving this course?

# Appendix E

## Online Technology Questionnaire

1. Where was the computer you used to access this course?
   O Home
   O Work
2. What browser did you use while accessing the course?
   O Netscape Communicator
   O Microsoft Internet Explorer
   O AOL
   O Other
3. Who was your Internet service provider (Earthlink, Bright.net, etc.)?
4. Please comment regarding the Internet connection made to this class via your Internet service provider (ISP) and any problems you may have had with it:
5. Were the assignment links relevant and easy to access?
   O Yes
   O No
6. If the assignment links were not relevant or easy to access, please explain:
7. Were the homework assignments easy to turn in?
   O Yes
   O No

8. Please comment regarding the WebCt homework/assignment drop box feature:

9. How many times did you use e-mail in WebCt?
   - O Never
   - O Once
   - O 2–5 times
   - O 6–10 times
   - O more than 10 times

10. Please comment on the WebCt email feature:

11. How many times did you use the bulletin board in WebCt?
    - O Never
    - O Once
    - O 2–5 times
    - O 6–10 times
    - O more than 10 times

12. Please comment on the WebCt bulletin board feature:

13. Please comment on the use of the WebCt chat room area:

14. What changes would you make to improve the course?

15. Finally, please make any comments regarding the technology used in this course and its effect on your learning experience:

# Glossary

**alternative instructional delivery:** The offering of classes in ways that do not require the physical presence of the learner and instructor in the same space at the same time to carry out the instructional processes (Ashland University Policy for Alternative Instructional Delivery, 2004).

**bulletin board:** Allows for information to be posted and for online discussions to take place based on predefined topic areas (WebCt, 2003).

**chat room:** Allows users to have real-time conversations with all of the users logged into the same server (WebCt, 2003).

**HTML (hypertext markup language):** The formatting language used for Web documents (Kearsley, 2000).

**links:** Allows the designer to add a link to either a local file or an external Uniform Resource Locator (URL) from a content model (WebCt, 2003).

**online course:** Teaching and learning takes place over a computer network such as the Internet in which interaction between people in an important form of support for the learning process (Howard, Schenk, & Discenza, 2004).

**server:** A computer that serves as the hub of a network (Kearsley, 2000).

**student-centered:** The instructor becomes a facilitator of information who stresses collaboration and independent student learning with the students becoming active participants (Knowlton, 2000).

**teacher-centered:** The instructor organizes the course, content, and learning activities without much input from the students (Knowlton, 2000).

**threaded discussions:** Allows users to engage in online discussions within predefined topic areas.

**uniform resource locator (URL):** Q Web address (WebCt, 2003).

**Web browser:** A program that allows access to the Web and reads HTML files such as Internet Explorer or Netscape Communications (Kearsley, 2000).

**Web-assisted courses:** Courses in which a substantial part of the instruction (30–70%) is carried out using Web-based materials and interaction (Ashland University Policy for Alternative Instructional Delivery, 2004).

**Web-based courses:** Courses in which most of the instruction in the class (more than 70 percent) is carried out using Web-based materials and interaction (Ashland University Policy for Alternative Instructional Delivery, 2004).

**Web-based materials:** Content materials that are found at a Web address (Ashland University Policy for Alternative Instructional Delivery, 2004).

**WebCt:** An e-learning system that allows the course designer to create an interactive learning environment that brings instructors and students together in a virtual classroom (WebCt, 2003).

# References

Academic community. Retrieved September 2, 2005, from www.section 508.gov/index.cfm?FuseAction=Content&ID=82.

Assistive technology showcase devices. Retrieved October 4, 2005, from www.section508.gov/index.cfm?FuseAction=Content&ID=87.

Anderson, R. G. (2001, November). *Adapting online courses to the curriculum of a traditional pedagogy, comprehensive liberal arts community: A case study on faculty roles and issues.* Paper presented at the meeting of the 2001 Computers on Campus National Conference, Myrtle Beach, SC.

*Ashland University Policy for alternative instructional delivery.* (2004, December). Ashland University Academic Affairs Standing Operating Procedures—Reference Section 14. Ashland, OH: Ashland University.

Bali, B. S., Moorman, M. S., Wingreen, S. J., & Adams, S. (2001, November). *Non-completion in alternative delivery courses: A two-year comparative study.* Paper presented at the meeting of 2001 Computers on Campus National Conference, Myrtle Beach, SC.

Bingham, J., Davis, T., & Moore, C. (1996). Emerging technology in distance learning. Retrieved 2001, October 8, from horizon.unc.edu/projects/ issues/papers/Distance_Learning.asp.

Boettcher, J. (1999). Nuggets about the shift to web-based teaching and learning. Retrieved August 10, 2001, from www.csus.edu/pedtech/ Nuggets.html.

Coomey, M. S., & Stephenson, J. (2002). Online learning: It is all about dialogue, involvement, support and control—according to research. In John Stephenson (Ed.), *Teaching & learning online: Pedagogies for new technologies.* London: Biddles Ltd.

Copyright Web site. Retrieved 2005, February 26, from www.benedict.com.

*Copyright & Ashland University.* (2004, July). Ashland, OH: Ashland University.

DeNigris, J., & Witchel, A. (2000). *How to teach and train online: Teaching the learning organization with tomorrow's tools today* (Rafferty, Ed.). Needham Heights, MA: Pearson.

Fink, L. D. (2003). Creating significant learning experiences: An integrated approach to designing college courses. San Francisco: Jossey-Bass.

Graham, C., Cagiltay, K., Lim, Byung-Ro, Craner, Joni, & Duffy, T. M. (2001, March/April). Seven principles of effective teaching: A practical lens for evaluating online courses. *The Technology Source.* Retrieved February 10, 2005, from mivu.org/default.asp?show=article&id=839.

Hanna, D. E., Glowacki-Dudka, M., & Conceição-Runlee. (2000). 147 practical tips for teaching online groups: Essentials of web-based education. Madison, WI: Atwood.

Harzari, S., & Schnorr, D. (1999, June 1). Leveraging student feedback to improve teaching in web-based courses. *T.H.E. Journal.* Retrieved February 4, 2005, from web23.epnet.com/citation.asp?tb=1&_ug=sid+ 26362E48%2D6.

How people with disabilities use the web. Retrieved September 27, 2005, from www.w3.org/WAI/EO/Drafts/PWD-Use-Web.

Howard, C., Schenk, K., & Discenza, R. (2004). Distance learning and university effectiveness: Changing educational paradigms for online learning. Hershey, PA: Information Science.

Instructional design resources. Retrieved February 15, 2005, from www.ion.uillinois.edu/resources/tutorials/id/index.asp.

Johnston, M., & Cooley, N. (2001, November/December). Toward more effective instructional uses of technology: The shift to virtual learning. *The Technology Source.* Retrieved December 10, 2004, from ts.mivu.org/ default.asp?show=article&id=869.

Kearsley, G. (2000). Online education: Learning and teaching in cyberspace. Toronto: Wadsworth.

Knowles, M. S. (1990). The adult learner: A neglected species (4th ed.). Houston: Gulf.

Knowlton, D. S. (2000). A theoretical framework for the online classroom: A defense and delineation of student-centered pedagogy. In R. E. Weiss, D. S. Knowlton, & B. W. Speck (Eds.), *New directions for teaching and learning: Principles of effective teaching in the online classroom* (pp. 5–13). (Vol. 84, Winter 2000). San Francisco: Jossey-Bass.

Lynch, M. M. (1998). Facilitating knowledge construction and communication on the internet. *The Technology Source.* (1998, December). Retrieved December 10, 2004, from www.horizon.unc.edu/TS/commentary/1998-12asp.

Noren, J. (1997). Andragogy: The teaching and learning of adults. Retrieved August 8, 1999, from www.park.edu/fac/facdev/noren.htm.

Palloff, R. M., & Pratt, K. (2005). Collaborating online: Learning together in community. San Francisco: Jossey-Bass.

Peters, L. (2001, September/October). Through the looking glass: Student perceptions of online learning. *The Technology Source.* Retrieved September 13, 2001, from http://www.horizon.unc.edu/TS/default.asp?show=article&id=907.

*Quality learning in Ohio and at a distance.* (2002, December). Ohio Learning Network. Columbus, OH: Ohio Learning Network.

Roblyer, M. D., & Ekhaml, L. (2000). How interactive are your distance courses? A rubric for assessing interaction in distance learning. Retrieved February 15, 2005, from www.westga.edu/~distance/roblyer32.html.

Senge, P. M. (1990). *The fifth discipline.* New York: Doubleday.

Staub, E. Interactive instructional designer. Retrieved February 15, 2005, from teir.osu.edu/acd.

*Strengths and weaknesses of alternatively delivered courses.* (2001, November). Minutes from the Alternative Instructional Delivery Committee. Ashland, OH: Ashland University.

Transformation tools for web content accessibility. Retrieved September 27, 2005, from www.w3.org/WAI/ER/existingtools.html.

UMUC-Verizon resources site for teaching with technology. Retrieved February 15, 2005, from www.umuc.eduvirualteaching/vt_home.html.

*WebCt—Getting started guide: WebCt campus education: 4.1.* (2003, August). Lynnfield, MA: WebCt.

Weiss, R. E. (2000). Humanizing the online classroom. In R. E. Weiss, D. S. Knowlton, & B. W. Speck (Eds.), *New directions for teaching and learning: Principles of effective teaching in the online classroom* (p. 51). (Vol. 84, Winter 2000). San Francisco: Jossey-Bass.

World lecture hall. Retrieved February 16, 2005, from web.austin.utexas.edu/wlh.